W9-BVV-727

Volume Three

Basics of Christian Thought

Todd Brennan, General Editor

THE PUZZLING GOSPELS

Suggested Explanations of
Puzzling Passages in
Matthew, Mark, Luke and John

Joseph Dahmus

THE THOMAS MORE PRESS
Chicago, Illinois

ISBN 0-88347-182-5

Publication of this volume of
BASICS OF CHRISTIAN THOUGHT
is made possible in part by a
ROBERT E. BURNS GRANT
from the Claretian Fathers and Brothers

Contents

FOREWORD

MORE books have been written about the Bible than on any other subject under the sun. In their unceasing efforts to unravel the mysteries of *the Good Book,* Biblical scholars have left little untouched and unexplained. Why then the need for this small volume? To do something these scholars have failed to do, that is, to compress into a short book answers to the questions about the gospels over which ordinary folk have usually puzzled.

Biblical scholars have not ignored these questions: their answers make up this book. But they have buried their answers to these simpler questions beneath reams of pages devoted to the explication of issues far beyond the needs or interests of the layperson. And few of these lay people have had the patience to search through the pages of their scholarly tomes for the answers they were seeking.

The ordinary lay person is not aware of the question whether the evangelist Matthew ever existed or not, for instance, or whether the author of "Q" used Matthew or did Matthew draw on "Q," or whether Matthew's gospel preceded in time, or followed, that of Mark, or what is meant by form criticism, or what the original language of the gospels may have been.

What he does puzzle over when he hears the gospel read to him on Sunday are simpler questions. Why, he asks himself, does Matthew trace Christ's genealogy through Joseph if Joseph was not the natural father of Jesus?

7

When Jesus' parents found him after three days in the Temple, why did he ask them why they had not realized he would be in his Father's house, and why did this explanation leave them wondering what it was all about? If Christ was the only child born to Mary, why the repeated references to Christ's brothers? Why did Christ seemingly work so many miracles on the Sabbath? Exactly what is the sense of the parable of the dishonest steward, the agent who arbitrarily remitted much of what his master's debtors owed and still received commendation for what he had done? Why did Christ first refuse, and rather brusquely at that, to consider the woman of Samaria's appeal that he cure her sick daughter, then warned his disciples to stay away from that part of Palestine?

Questions of this kind, not those of a textual or metaphysical nature that worry only biblical scholars, haunt church-goers as they return to their homes after Sunday service. The minister or priest may not have had, or may not have taken, the time to explain the puzzling passages.

Since the gospel according to Matthew is the longest, is judged the most complete, and is at the same time, probably the most familiar of the four gospels, problems such as those suggested above will be considered first in the sequence in which they come to view in his work, accompanied with references to parallel passages in Mark, Luke and John. Problems which are individual to the other evangelists will then come in for consideration.

The passages cited are from *The New Oxford Annotated Bible with the Apocrypha.* Revised Standard Version. Edited by Herbert G. May and Bruce M. Metzger. New York: Oxford University Press, 1973. (An Ecumenical Study Bible.)

THE GOSPEL ACCORDING TO MATTHEW

THE very first chapter of the gospel according to Matthew gives Christians something to puzzle over. At the beginning of his gospel Matthew introduces Christ to his readers by tracing his ancestry from Abraham, the traditional progenitor of the Hebrew people. He carries this genealogy all the way down to Joseph, the husband of Mary. Those Christians who believe Christ had no earthly father may well ask, why trace Christ's ancestry through Joseph if Joseph was not his father?

The passage reads:

THE BOOK OF THE GENEALOGY OF JESUS CHRIST, the son of David, the son of Abraham. Abraham was the father of Isaac, and Isaac the father of Jacob, and Jacob the father of Judah and his brothers, and Judah the father of Perez and Zerah by Tamar, and Perez the father of Hezron . . . and Jacob the father of Joseph the husband of Mary, of whom Jesus was born, who is called Christ (Matthew 1:1-3, 16). See Luke 3:23-38.

This passage is part of the genealogy of Christ as given by Matthew in the opening chapter of his gospel. The final statement that inserts the name of Joseph in this genealogy poses the question: since most Christians believe Christ had no natural father, why trace his ancestry through Joseph?

The explanation is a relatively simple one. According to Jewish law of the time, fatherhood was a legal, not necessarily a physical, matter. Once a man had acknowledged a child to be his own, natural or otherwise, no further ques-

9

tion remained concerning their relationship. Christ's contemporaries, including those who had grown up with him in Nazareth and who knew him best, accepted him as the son of Joseph, the carpenter. While the evangelists who penned their gospels some thirty-five or more years later did not view Joseph as Christ's natural father, in tracing our Lord's genealogy and his descent from David they listed Joseph, since he was Christ's legal parent.

Several minor difficulties remain concerning the question of Christ's genealogy. That the Jacob mentioned by Matthew as the father of Joseph was probably childless is disturbing even though one must not expect complete historical accuracy in any of the gospels. (The genealogies of Matthew and Luke reveal more discrepancies than they do agreement.) Jacob may have adopted Joseph or, failing that, Joseph could have claimed descent from David through his natural father, Heli, as given in Luke 3:23. In any event, Joseph stood in the line of David, either through Jacob or Heli or through both of them, and that was the principal reason for his being listed among Christ's ancestors. (See Matthew 1:20, where the angel addresses Joseph as "son of David," and below, p.12.)

Christian scholars as early as the fifth century, in an effort to remove any doubts concerning Christ's divine parentage, inserted the name of Joachim as Mary's reputed father, in the genealogical table after the name of Joseph as given in Luke. Not only does the name of Joachim not appear in the oldest manuscripts of Luke, but those apologists, in thus deliberately altering the text, left themselves the problem of establishing Mary's (Joachim's) descent from David. For this there exists no scriptural evidence. Christ was of the line of David through Joseph, not through Mary.

The problem of establishing Mary's descent from David also saddles those more recent scholars who interpret Luke 3:23 ("Jesus, when he began his ministry, was about thirty years of age, being the son (as was supposed) of Joseph, the son of Heli") in a way that would eliminate Joseph in reckoning Christ's genealogy. Their reasoning, that Joseph was only supposed to have been Christ's father, is forced at best; at worst it violates the practice of the time which traced parentage through the man, in this case, through Joseph, whom contemporaries recognized as the father. Furthermore, the angel who appeared in a dream to assure him that it was quite proper for him to take Mary home as his wife, instructed him, "You shall call his name Jesus" (Matthew 1:21). The act of Joseph in giving the child Jesus his own name counted as legal adoption and thereby established Christ's descent from David.

Several exegetes suggest that Matthew introduced the name of Mary in his genealogy because he believed her to be the mother of Christ, not through Joseph, but by the instrumentality of the Holy Spirit.

*   *   *

IMMEDIATELY after giving the account of Christ's genealogy, Matthew says something regarding the relationship
between Joseph and Mary, prior to the birth of Jesus that
is startling. It sounds as if Joseph wanted to be rid of
Mary!

The passage reads:

> Now the birth of Jesus Christ took place in this way.
> When his mother Mary had been betrothed to Joseph,
> before they came together she was found to be with
> child of the Holy Spirit; and her husband Joseph, being
> a just man and unwilling to put her to shame, resolved
> to divorce her quietly. But as he considered this, behold,
> an angel of the Lord appeared to him in a dream, say-
> ing, "Joseph, son of David, do not fear to take Mary as
> your wife, for that which is conceived in her is of the
> Holy Spirit; she will bear a son, and you shall call his
> name Jesus, for he will save his people from their sins."
> All this took place to fulfill what the Lord had spoken
> by the prophet: "Behold, a virgin shall conceive and
> bear a son, and his name shall be called Emmanuel"
> (which means, God with us). When Joseph woke from
> sleep, he did as the angel of the Lord commanded him;
> he took his wife, but knew her not until she had borne a
> son; and he called his name Jesus (Matthew 1:18-25).

This passage raises several questions. Why, for instance,
did Mary fail to tell Joseph of the visit of the angel Gabriel,
the divine messenger, when he announced she would con-
ceive and have a child through the Holy Spirit (Luke
1:34-35)? Was it humility or modesty that kept her silent
about so important a matter, or did she actually give
Joseph this information? Luke says nothing of the di-

lemma in which Joseph found himself, neither do Mark and John.

If one holds to a strict reading of the text, each of the following conclusions may be accepted: first, that Joseph had no knowledge of Gabriel's visit to Mary; second, that he had had no carnal knowledge of Mary when he learned that she was with child and, third, that he assumed Mary was with child by another man, yet rather than subject her to a public trial and possible penalties, decided to dismiss her privately.

The interpretation of the passage turns upon the manner one understands the words: "Joseph, being a just man . . ." Commentators disagree. One will argue that since Joseph was a just man, he decided, in the hope of shielding Mary, to put her away privately without offering any specific reason for doing so. This was possible according to Jewish practice. Another commentator will argue that since Joseph was a just man, he felt obliged to obey the law. This left him a choice of either dismissing Mary when he discovered her to be pregnant or of citing her before a tribunal and seeing her punished; that being both a man of honor and upright as well, he was unwilling to expose Mary and so chose to divorce her privately, probably in the presence of her parents as the law would have allowed.

While this line of action would leave Mary in some disgrace once the child was born, the alternative was a public trial in the presence of three rabbis, when proven delinquency on Mary's part would have left her liable to severe penalties. It has also been suggested that the "justice" of Joseph prevented him from posing as the father of the child to be born, when he was not.

Some commentators take the position that because Joseph was a just man he did not wish to divorce Mary publicly since he was himself convinced she was innocent of any sexual irregularity. In somewhat similar fashion argue other scholars who maintain that Joseph was convinced Mary's pregnancy had come by supernatural intervention and for that reason felt unworthy to take her to be his wife. He therefore decided to put her away quietly.

While these commentators interpret the passage in a manner that does honor to both Joseph and Mary, their lines of reasoning may have the opposite result. Had Joseph decided not to marry Mary because of his great reverence for her, his action would have left her open to public ridicule once the child was born, something he could have prevented, but for his insistence on being a just man or as a person unworthy of her.

If Joseph was the upright man Matthew says he was and if his sense of honor had not prevented him, he would surely have been willing to accept the child to be born as his own in order to spare Mary the dishonor of being an unwed mother. Even if Joseph believed, or had been so informed by heaven, that Mary had conceived by some supernatural means and for that reason felt unworthy to have her as his wife, people would have not shared that conviction. They would have judged her to be a fornicator (adultress) and her child a bastard. All Matthew probably wanted to say is that, in divorcing Mary, Joseph wished to avoid accusing her of adultery. Such action would have forced a public trial.

According to Jewish custom of the time, the girl who had been betrothed remained in the home of her parents for as much as ten months or even longer before the nuptials were celebrated, at which time her husband would take her to his house and consummate the marriage. Until that time the two were only betrothed, not married. Yet so binding was the nature of this agreement that unfaithfulness during the interval prior to the actual ceremony was judged tantamount to adultery. It was during this interval that Joseph somehow learned that Mary was pregnant.

The reading in a number of English editions of the text in Isaiah 7:14 speaks of a young woman rather than a virgin conceiving and bearing a son. The original Hebrew lends itself to either translation. Matthew prefers to translate it with virgin.

The text that tells how Joseph, when awakened from his sleep, did as the angel had instructed, took Mary as his wife, but he "knew her not until she had borne a son," has stirred much controversy. It implies, or may imply, that Joseph did live with Mary as husband. The more common translation of this passage, that Joseph had no relations with Mary until she had borne her "first-born son," appears to confirm the implication.

To those Christians who believe Mary had a number of children after Jesus, as the usual translation of the Greek seems to suggest, this passage in Matthew occasions no difficulty. For others it does, notably for Roman Catholics who believe that Mary remained a virgin throughout her life. The question of Mary's perpetual virginity remains a problem and one that will receive extended consideration later. (See below, pp. 54-58.) Here a word of caution will suffice about the danger of giving ancient terms the translation which presumably means the same in our modern languages. Even the "awful" of Shakespeare's day has acquired a meaning he knew nothing about.

The word *until* in the sentence telling how Joseph did not have sexual relations with Mary "until she had borne a son" may mean what our *until* does today, but it need not. Matthew, in any case, was not concerned about any future children Mary might have had. He wanted to make two things clear: first, that Joseph had no relations with Mary before Christ was born and that the child born to her was therefore of divine origin; second, that Mary was still a virgin when Christ was born and, accordingly, met the requirement laid down by Isaiah about a virgin giving birth to a son whom they would call Emmanuel.

The word *first-born* also poses some difficulty. Most commentators agree that the implication modern readers are apt to attach to it, namely, that Mary had children in addition to Jesus, did not hold for biblical times. Here it is simply employed as a Semitic legal term to emphasize the fact that since Jesus was the first-born male, he was to be considered specially consecrated to God, which fact also left the parents under the obligations described in Luke 2:22-24, when they brought him to the Temple and offered a pair of doves. St. Jerome, in commenting on this passage, points out that every only child is a first-born child, but not every first-born is an only child. It does happen that several of the ancient manuscripts leave out the word *first-born*.

*   *   *

IN the frequent confrontations between Christ and the Pharisees, no one issue set them more regularly at odds than the law of Moses and its interpretation. Not that Christ did not know the law and all the manifold disciplinary practices and regulations as well that had come to supplement it since the days of Moses. Christ and the Pharisees did not differ as to how the law read. They disagreed as to how it should be interpreted and applied. In the passage cited below, Christ is also objecting to the many accretions to the law that had accumulated over the centuries and, in the judgment of the legalistic-minded Pharisees, had received the sanction of law. As Christ maintained, he had not come to destroy the law. His faith was sprung from the law of the Old Testament. He could not disavow it nor would he. Still, times change and with time laws may lose their reasonableness unless they receive constant reinterpretation and application. In the passage below Christ is attacking in particular the practice of rabbis to refine the law of Moses to a point where it no longer made sense.

The passage reads:

"Think not that I have come to abolish the law and the prophets. I have come not to abolish them but to fulfill them. For truly, I say to you, till heaven and earth pass away, not an iota, not a dot, will pass from the law until all is accomplished. Whoever then relaxes one of the least of these commandments and teaches men so, shall be called least in the kingdom of heaven; but he who does them and teaches them shall be called great in the kingdom of heaven" (Matthew 5:17-19).

The statement of Christ may refer to the practice Jewish

rabbis had of identifying 613 commandments in the law and of dividing these into two groups, those that were of major importance and those of minor importance. Christ rejected any such distinction together with the tendency it could easily encourage of paying little or no attention to the commandments of lesser importance. Jesus does not say that one who ignores the lesser commandments and teaches others to do likewise will be rejected. That person will be called but will be assigned the lowest place. That person will be judged great in the kingdom, on the other hand, who observes all commandments, including the relatively unimportant, and teaches others to follow his example.

*   *   *

CHRIST proved himself a great teacher and an eloquent preacher. If he hoped to get his message across, he had no choice but to be both. The people he spoke to were largely illiterate, and he had little time in which to instruct them. Only a few could he expect to see a second time. He must keep to the point in his preaching; he must employ colorful language, striking metaphors, and other rhetorical devices in the hopes of arousing and holding their attention, and he must leave them thoughts and ideas to take home with them that they would not easily forget. In the passage below, he goes so far as to direct his listeners to maim themselves, even to tear out their eyes, in order to avoid sin.

The passage reads:

> "You have heard that it was said, 'You shall not commit adultery.' But I say to you that every one who looks at a woman lustfully has already committed adultery with her in his heart. If your right eye causes you to sin, pluck it out and throw it away; it is better that you lose one of your members than that your whole body be thrown into hell. And if your right hand causes you to sin, cut it off and throw it away; it is better that you lose one of your members than that your whole body go into hell" (Matthew 5:27-30).

If this passage that appears twice in Matthew (see 18:8-9) and again in Mark (9:43-47) were to receive a literal interpretation, the world might be filled with one-eyed, one-armed people, and even worse. Since the passage may be interpreted as implying that the remaining eye or hand should also be destroyed if they were the occasion of sin, a literal application of this exhortation would leave the world populated with blind, armless people.

Christ's language is figurative. He did not intend men and women to mutilate themselves. What he aimed to do was to curb sins of impurity, and it was in this connection that he issued this warning. What he is doing here is employing a sort of surgical metaphor, as one commentator put it, to the end that just as it may be necessary to cut off a diseased hand in order to save a man's life, so a similarly painful expedient may be necessary, such as the practice of the most severe kind of self-discipline, in order to save a person's soul.

It should be noted that Christ gave added emphasis to his admonition by recommending the amputation of the right hand rather than the left, since for most people the right is considered more valuable.

* * *

IN our lawyer-ridden world of today with its bulging docket of court cases it is difficult to imagine Christ ever proposing a society that would get along without oaths. According to Matthew, it was that kind of world that he hoped to establish.

The passage reads:

> "Again you have heard that it was said to the men of old, 'You shall not swear falsely, but shall perform to the Lord what you have sworn.' But I say to you, do not swear at all, either by heaven, for it is the throne of God, or by the earth, for it is his footstool, or by Jerusalem, for it is the city of the great King. And do not swear by your head, for you cannot make one hair white or black. Let what you say be simply 'Yes' or 'No'; anything more than this comes from evil" (Matthew 5:33-37).

Here again, as in the instance of an offending eye (see above, p. 19), we have an illustration of Christ's willingness to overstate a counsel in order to emphasize the necessity of correcting a practice that had become common for Jews, namely, that of confirming almost every firm statement with an oath. The Jews were also wont to draw a fine legal distinction regarding the relative value and sanctity of oaths sworn in different ways, e.g., by the kingdom of God, by the earth, by Jerusalem.

Christ condemned all oath-taking whatever the presumed justification since man as the creature of God is always under obligation to tell the truth. An oath at best is a compromise with a sinful world and a concession to the devil, the father of lies. As for distinguishing between the binding character of different oaths, that was blasphemous in itself since the fact of calling on God to bear witness outweighed in an infinite measure by whatever appeal a particular oath might be confirmed.

Certain Christian sects have scrupulously respected Christ's injunction against oath-taking, not so Christian society in general. It was, indeed, the very respect in which oaths were held that invested such medieval methods of ascertaining guilt as the ordeal and compurgation with what effectiveness they possessed. St. Louis IX of France (d.1270) never affirmed anything more positively than with a "Truly it was thus" or "Truly it shall be thus."

* * *

THROUGHOUT history pacifism as a gospel to prevent war has attracted many advocates. Here Christ is proposing a kind of pacifism that few individuals other than the genuinely Christian, have made any serious effort to adopt.

The passage reads:

"You have heard that it was said, 'An eye for an eye and a tooth for a tooth.' But I say to you, Do not resist one who is evil. But if any one strikes you on the right cheek, turn to him the other also; and if any one would sue you and take your coat, let him have your cloak as well; and if any one forces you to go one mile, go with him two miles" (Matthew 5:38-41). See Luke 6:29.

Christ's intent in expressing this counsel was to correct a kind of behavior that appeared prescribed in the law of Moses, that is "an eye for an eye and a tooth for a tooth" (Exodus 21:24; Leviticus 24:20; Deuteronomy 19:21). Again Christ overstates his instruction in order to give it greater force. He surely did not intend his listeners to turn the other cheek to the assailant who had struck him, if for no other reason than that would have aggravated the offense of the attacker.

A literal application of Christ's counsel as recorded in both Matthew and Luke (6:29) would have men and women shedding all their clothes and going naked, something again Jesus certainly did not contemplate.

The instruction about going two miles if one should insist upon the disciple's going one refers to the forced service that the Romans in Palestine compelled Jews to render when soldiers or officials were passing through: e.g., to carry baggage and other impedimenta. Christ tells his disciples to accept such demands and even to offer to do twice what was ordered.

When Christ speaks of the right rather than left cheek he may have in mind the possibility that a backhanded blow on the right cheek was deemed particularly insulting, or that the right cheek, just as the right eye and the right hand (see above, p. 19) was considered the more important. The coat, mentioned by Luke, was a long undergarment with sleeves; the cloak a sort of blanket or cape worn over this which served the poor as a coverlet at night. A plaintiff could sue for the coat but not for the cloak.

The moral of Christ's instructions is that the disciple is not to permit selfishness or anger to determine the nature of his response to mistreatment or to unreasonable demands. While Christ's direction suggests the ideal, it would be a sorry world were everyone to insist upon his rights as he viewed them or returned violence for violence and injury for injury. His words recommend a generosity that is willing to go beyond that which is necessary, but a generosity that experience has shown will more often than not evoke a generous response and thus contribute in the end to greater tranquility and peace. It suggests the kind of behavior that marks, or should mark, the contrast between a Christian and a pagan society.

* * *

THE God-fearing individual who insists he needs no church but does well enough praying alone will defend his position on the basis of the following passage from Matthew.

The passage reads:

"And when you pray, you must not be like the hypocrites; for they love to stand and pray in the synagogues and at the street corners, that they may be seen by men. Truly, I say to you, they have received their reward. But when you pray, go into your room and shut the door and pray to your Father who is in secret; and your Father who sees in secret will reward you" (Matthew 6:5-6).

The point of this counsel stands clearly revealed in the opening verse: "And when you pray, you must not be like the hypocrites; for they love to stand and pray in the synagogues and at the street corners." Christ does not condemn "public" prayer, only ostentation and insincerity when addressing the Father. Any prayer to the Father must come from the heart, and this kind of prayer is pleasing to God whether said in private or offered by a group. See Matthew 18:20, where Christ promises to be in the midst of the "two or three" who gather in his name.

There is a time and place for both private and public prayer. That person errs who lets one of Christ's counsels guide him while ignoring a kindred one with which it must be associated. Most theologians maintain that the most efficacious prayers are those offered by the church community since Christ continues to live in the church which he founded.

* * *

MATTHEW has Christ giving more advice on the subject of prayer, and what he says may leave many wondering whether a short prayer might be as efficacious in winning God's favor as a longer or oft-repeated one.

The passage reads:

> "And in praying do not heap up empty phrases as the Gentiles do for they think that they will be heard for their many words. Do not be like them, for your Father knows what you need before you ask him. Pray then like this: Our father who art in heaven . . ." (Matthew 6:7-9).

What Christ had in mind were the repeated phrases or epithets that pagans were wont to babble in their prayers to their god(s) in order to make sure that among those they rattled off would be the precise one that most pleased the deity. Christ appears to intimate that the Father liked short, simple prayers, for he followed up the above instruction with the counsel: "Do not be like them, for your Father knows what you need before you ask him." Then he taught his disciples the relatively short, concise Lord's Prayer.

Babbling prayerful phrases in a mindless sort of way is not to be confused with prayers repeated in all sincerity and fervor. Christ tells of a widow whose persistent entreaties so wore down a harsh judge's patience that he finally gave her what she wanted. His followers should be as persistent with their prayers to God. (See Luke 18:1-8.) Christ himself thrice repeated his prayer to the Father in Gethsemane to be spared the crucifixion (Matthew 26: 38-44).

* * *

THE virtues and powers that Christians attribute to their God and those that Moslems ascribe to Allah leave these deities largely similar. A significant difference between the responsiveness of the God of the Christians and the Allah of the Moslems comes to view, however, in the promise of Christ, given here in Matthew, that whoever asks will receive and who seeks will find. No such promise is found in the Koran. Moslems who respect Allah's commands will enjoy the happiness of Paradise, those who do not will be damned.

The passage from Matthew reads:

"Ask, and it will be given you; seek, and you will find; knock, and it will be opened to you. For every one who asks receives, and he who seeks finds, and to him who knocks it will be opened. Or what man of you, if his son asks him for bread, will give him a stone? Or if he asks for a fish, will give him a serpent? If you then, who are evil, know how to give good gifts to your children, how much more will your Father who is in heaven give good things to those who ask him!" (Matthew 7:7-11).

This same counsel appears again in Matthew 21:22, also in Mark 11:24, Luke 11:9-13, and John 16:23. That all four evangelists record this same promise is understandable since it is probably the one Christians find most appealing, and for the majority of people a more tangible reward for observing God's commandments than the promise of ultimate happiness in the hereafter.

At first glance, Christ appears to commit the Father to answering any prayer, whatever the nature of the petition. This is manifestly impossible. God would surely not honor the prayer of one who sought to do injury to a neighbor, neither would he grant eternal youthfulness to the vain person who begged for it. There clearly exists some limitation to the Father's receptivity, and the nature of this limitation is implied in Matthew 6:7 where Christ tells his listeners that the Father knew what they needed before they asked. (See above, p. 26.) And John (1 John 5:14) writes: "And this is the confidence which we have in him, that if we ask anything according to his will he hears us." So what the Christian asks of the Father must, above all other considerations, be something God feels he needs.

On the strength of a text in Luke (11:13), namely, "If you then, who are evil, know how to give good gifts to your children, how much more will the heavenly Father give the Holy Spirit to those who ask him!" one might conclude that what Christ wanted his listeners to ask for above all else was the Holy Spirit. Nothing other could compare in value with that gift, while a truly devout Christian, a saint, one with the faith to move mountains (see below, 73) would hesitate to ask for anything less.

Other prayers that Christ recommended also had a spiritual objective, e.g., when he told his disciples to ask the Father to send laborers into his harvest (Matthew 9:38), when he explained that only prayer could dislodge a particularly vicious demon (Mark 9:29), and when, in Gethsemane, he warned his apostles to pray lest they fall into temptation (Luke 22:40). On the other hand, Christ in hearkening to the prayers of the sick, the blind, and the crippled demonstrated that God would also show himself responsive to prayers for material blessings.

Christ urged his listeners not to give up hope over unanswered prayers but "that they ought always to pray and not lose heart." When his disciples asked him to teach them how to pray he told them about a man who came to the house of a friend at midnight and asked for food, was refused because the door had been barred and the children were asleep, but how after repeated requests the friend finally relented and opened the door (Luke 11:5-8). Again, Christ told a parable about a widow who importuned an arrogant judge so much about giving her justice that he finally granted her request, "or she will wear me out by her continual coming" (Luke 18:1-7). And Christ himself in Gethsemane thrice repeated the prayer to the Father to be spared the Passion (Matthew 26:39-44). It may even happen that some time after a person has given up praying for a certain thing, he finds himself relieved that God had not answered his prayer.

Christ's assurance regarding the Father's willingness to answer prayers should be interpreted as applying, first, to prayers that are reasonable and, second, to prayers whose fulfillment would be beneficial, especially in terms of spiritual values. Another way of stating this is to say that a prayer that goes unanswered is one whose fulfillment, under the circumstances, would serve neither our best interests nor those of others. On the principle that any petition to God—that is, a turning to him—is a good in itself, all ministers and priests assure the faithful that no prayer is ever wasted, that is, never goes without notice.

* * *

HOW difficult is the task of saving one's soul? Of the billions of humans who have lived on this planet, how many will make it to heaven? This is a question that many God-fearing persons have asked themselves, and what Christ affirmed on that problem, as recorded by Matthew, is not reassuring.

The passage reads:

> "Enter by the narrow gate; for the gate is wide and the way is easy, that leads to destruction, and those who enter by it are many. For the gate is narrow and the way is hard, that leads to life, and those who find it are few" (Matthew 7:13-14).

If Christ appears here to be warning his listeners that few will be able to find and pass through the narrow gate that leads to heaven, that warning should be weighed against the words he addressed to his disciples on this same subject on a later occasion. He had just commented on the difficulty rich men would have in getting to heaven (see below, p. 78), an observation that prompted his disciples to ask, in seeming desperation, whether anyone could possibly be saved, so severe were heaven's demands. Christ's answer was a simple: "With men this is impossible, but for God all things are possible" (Matthew 19:26).

There have been learned and saintly people who have maintained that few people will be saved, also learned and saintly people who have insisted that most people will gain salvation. It is well to keep in mind that Christ was first and last a teacher, that he was speaking to men and women who were quite immature as far as their ability to comprehend spiritual truths was concerned. For this reason, and like any good teacher, in order to emphasize a point, Christ was willing to overstate the case.

* * *

THE disease of leprosy was well-known in biblical times
and the evangelists record a number of occasions when
Christ miraculously cleansed lepers of this terrible malady.
On one of these occasions Matthew tells how Christ, after
having healed a leper, ordered him not to publicize his
good fortune but to keep it to himself. The injunction may
strike the reader as strange since it was by means of
miracles that Christ could most convincingly confirm the
divine nature of his mission.

The passage reads:

> When he came down from the mountain, great crowds
> followed him and behold, a leper came to him and knelt
> before him, saying, "Lord, if you will, you can make me
> clean." And he stretched out his hand and touched him,
> saying, "I will; be clean." And immediately his leprosy
> was cleansed. And Jesus said to him, "See that you say
> nothing to any one; but go, show yourself to the priest,
> and offer the gift that Moses commanded, for a proof to
> the people" (Matthew 8:1-4).

Why did Christ direct the man to tell no one of the miracle that had cleansed him of his leprosy? The usual explanation is that in ordering the ex-leper to present himself
immediately to the priests and to speak to no one on the
way, Christ was but showing his respect for the law of
Moses which prescribed that procedure (Leviticus 14:2).
Was the man free to make public the fact of his having
been cleansed after he had reported the matter to the
priests? It appears that Christ's instructions did not extend
beyond the point of the ex-leper's speaking to the priests.
In all probability the ex-leper would return to the home he
had left, to his relatives and friends, when the fact of his

having been cleansed would have spoken louder than words. This was something Christ could not have prevented had he wished; in fact, he advised the man from whom he had exorcized a demon: "Go home to your friends, and tell them how much the Lord has done for you, and how he has had mercy on you" (Mark 5:19).

There are other passages in the gospels, however, that have Christ instructing the beneficiaries of his miracles to keep silent about the matter. He ordered the blind man to whom he had given sight to go to his house but to tell no one in the village what had happened (Mark 8:26), while the deaf man, now hearing, was strictly charged to keep silent about the miracle Christ had worked for him (Mark 7:36). An even more striking instance of Christ's wish to limit or even suppress the knowledge of his miracles is provided by Matthew (12:15-16), who reports that Christ, after curing many people, ordered "them not to make him known." (See also Matthew 9:27-31.)

One may find an explanation in Mark 1:45, why Christ may have wished to keep quiet the news about his miracles. The evangelist writes that when the leper whom Christ had cured failed to heed his order to remain silent about the miracle but went out and blazed it abroad, Christ could no longer go openly into any town but kept himself to desert places. People were hunting him down, not to hear what he had to preach, but out of curiosity, to see the wonderworker. Between this idle curiosity and the demands people would be making upon him to cure them of their maladies, there would be little time left for teaching and preaching. It was for this reason, too, that Christ directed the demons he had driven out of the possessed not to reveal his identity as the son of God (Mark 3:12).

Some commentators suggest that what prompted Jesus

to order the leper made clean not to publicize that fact but to report immediately to the priests was the fear lest Christ's enemies prevent the man from doing so, possibly even doing him physical injury should he so wish. The possibility has even been suggested that the priests, out of hostility for Christ, would conspire to deny a cure had taken place should the knowledge of a particular miracle reach them before the ex-leper. Christ's instruction to the leper to tell no one but to take himself without delay to the priests may also have carried an indirect caution for the leper lest he grow proud through repeated telling of the amazing blessing bestowed upon him.

*   *   *

CHRIST quite regularly referred to himself as the Son of Man. Matthew and the other evangelists record the title but offer no explanation as to its precise significance.

The passage reads:

And a scribe came up and said to him, "Teacher, I will follow you wherever you go." And Jesus said to him, "Foxes have holes, and birds of the air have nests; but the Son of Man has nowhere to lay his head" (Matthew 8:19-20).

The title, Son of Man, was Christ's favorite way of referring to himself. It appears thirty-one times in Matthew; fourteen times in Mark; twenty-five times in Luke; and thirteen times in John. Much learned discussion has been offered to explain its meaning. The title also appears many times in the Old Testament, about eighty times in Ezekiel alone, where it receives varying interpretations.

Most commentators consider it a Messianic title, and it was recognized as such by the Jews in Christ's day. Where it appears in the gospels, it is usually assumed to refer to the human nature in Christ, although this never apart from his divinity, and, more specifically, to refer to the humility of the mission he undertook in obedience to the will of the Father. It emphasized, therefore, the role of Christ in bringing salvation. In the above text from Matthew, it suggests Christ's humble, homeless lot. In other passages in the gospels the title may imply Christ's mission of suffering and death, even his final triumph and glory.

* * *

ON one occasion, a young man came to Jesus and asked to
be his follower, his disciple, although he was not ready to
leave with him immediately. Christ was willing to accept
the young man, but he would not tolerate any delay. Is it
possible to charge Christ with impatience, even with harshness, if we are to take Matthew literally?

The passage reads:

> Another of the disciples said to him, "Lord, let me first
> go and bury my father." But Jesus said to him, "Follow
> me, and leave the dead to bury their own dead" (Mat-
> thew 8:21–22).

The Greek text fails to make clear whether the father
was already dead or simply far advanced in years. In the
latter case, the would-be disciple was asking Christ to permit him to remain with his father during his last days. The
point that Christ wished to make, in any event, was that
when one wishes to serve God, all other considerations,
even responsibilities to one's family, must give way.

The parallel passage in Luke (9:59–62) suggests that interpretation. It reads: "To another he said, 'Follow me.'
But he said, 'Lord, let me first go and bury my father.' But
he said to him, 'Leave the dead to bury their own dead; but
as for you, go and proclaim the kingdom of God.'"

If Christ's instruction sounds harsh to us, it must have
actually shocked his Jewish listeners since they possessed
an unusually high respect for the obligation of filial piety
to one's aged parents. Here again, as later when Christ
seems to urge his listeners to hate their parents (see below,
p. 127), it may be a case of Christ's overstating a point in
the hope of leaving a lasting impression. He surely did not
wish to imply that anyone who refused to be his disciple is

dead, spiritually speaking, rather that anyone who has received the call, since it is the most worthy of all calls a person may receive, should give that message precedence over any other obligation. Let those who have not received the call to serve a higher cause perform the ordinary duties of family and society. What Christ is recommending, in effect, is the ideal, a choice that was open only to those who wished to be perfect.

Christ's seemingly harsh words may also hold the intended meaning that whoever does not recognize the prior claim of the kingdom of God, a claim that takes precedence even over family obligations, is spiritually dead and may be left to bury the (physically) dead. Finally, of a simpler nature is the explanation that Christ was urging the would-be disciple to leave others, those who had not received the call, to bury his father when he died. Should the young man remain behind to await his father's death, he would find Christ long departed from that region since he was already on the point of leaving. Once Christ was no longer in the vicinity, the would-be disciple might well change his mind and give up all thought of joining Christ.

Christ's admonition may carry a symbolic meaning. He may have been advising the would-be disciple to leave a dying cause, that is, Israel of the Old Covenant or perhaps even that of John the Baptist, and join him in spreading the new gospel.

* * *

ONE would conclude from reading the gospels, that diabolical possession was not uncommon in biblical times. Matthew relates an instance of such possession although this one has a curious twist.

The passage reads:

> And when he came to the other side, to the country of the Gadarenes, two demoniacs met him, coming out of the tombs, so fierce that no one could pass that way. And behold, they cried out, "What have you to do with us, O Son of God? Have you come here to torment us before the time?" Now a herd of many swine was feeding at some distance from them. And the demons begged him, "If you cast us out, send us away into the herd of swine." And he said to them, "Go." So they came out and went into the swine; and behold, the whole herd rushed down the steep bank into the sea, and perished in the waters (Matthew 8:28-32).

Some critics may be inclined to fault Christ for being instrumental in the destruction of the herd of swine. If so, they may draw comfort from the possibility that the owners of the hogs were Hebrews, in which case they were doing what for them was illegal. This is only a possibility, however, since the region was probably Gentile or at least so in part. On the other hand, if Christ's action in apparently allowing the destruction of the herd of pigs should strike the modern reader as strange, if not reprehensible, he should bear in mind that people in biblical times were less sensitive about the "rights" of animals than we are.

Why the demons wished permission to take refuge in the hogs is not explained. The hogs may perhaps have afforded them an immediate place to stay until something more to their liking presented itself. The Jews would have considered swine a most fitting place for demons since these animals were considered to be unclean.

Matthew does not say specifically that Christ permitted the demons to enter the swine. To their request to do this, his answer was a simple, "Go." Mark 5:1-13 and Luke 8:27-33 have Christ giving the demons this permission.

* * *

THE relationship between Christ and John the Baptist remains one of the more intriguing facets of the gospel story. Did John and Jesus ever meet again after Christ's baptism? What was the nature of John's preaching? Even if he recognized Christ as the Son of God, a man whose sandals he was not worthy to loose (Mark 1:7), he apparently did not join Christ in the latter's mission. In fact, as Matthew tells of the incident, he had his own disciples, and there must have been occasions when differences in what they preached or in their disciplines strained relations between them. Matthew tells of one such incident.

The passage reads:

> Then the disciples of John came to him, saying, "Why do we and the Pharisees fast, but your disciples do not fast?" And Jesus said to them, "Can the wedding guests mourn as long as the bridegroom is with them. The days will come, when the bridegroom is taken away from them, and then they will fast" (Matthew 9:14-15).

One may not conclude from the above text that the disciples did no fasting prior to Christ's crucifixion. Among the different instructions he preached to the people and to his disciples in the Sermon on the Mount was the reminder: "But when you fast, anoint your head and wash your face, that your fasting may not be seen by men but by your Father who is in secret; and your Father who sees in secret will reward you" (Matthew 6:16-18).

Is it possible that the disciples fasted in so unobtrusive a manner as to leave others unaware of that fact? More likely it was simply that their manner of fasting was less methodical and regulated than that of the Pharisees and John's disciples.

Christ's own action in fasting for forty days in the desert before embarking on his ministry (Matthew 4:1-2) makes clear the importance he attached to such self-discipline. Again, on the occasion when his disciples confessed their inability to drive out a particularly stubborn demon, Christ emphasized the importance of fasting. He warned them that only prayer and fasting could dislodge so vicious a devil (Mark 9:29).

While Christ did not rule out all fasting in his answer to John's disciples, what he intended to do was to announce the dawn of a new age, the Messianic age, which was to be considered distinct from the old dispensation. Jesus and his disciples were the messengers of the good news; theirs was a religion of joy; theirs was a different world from that of the Old Law.

The law of Moses did not actually require the frequent fasting that the Pharisees and John's disciples practiced. Christ was breaking with the oral tradition that prescribed this kind of excessive fasting.

* * *

HOW different was the gospel that Christ preached from what the scribes and Pharisees accepted as the true religion? This passage in Matthew leaves the impression that the two, Christ's gospel and the Judaism practiced by the Pharisees, were irreconcilable. To make this point clear, Christ employs one of his most striking images.

The passage reads:

> "And no one puts a piece of unshrunk cloth on an old garment, for the patch tears away from the garment, and a worse tear is made. Neither is new wine put into old wineskins; if it is, the skins burst, and the wine is spilled, and the skins are destroyed; but new wine is put into fresh wineskins, and so both are preserved" (Matthew 9:16-17).

Christ used a fact of common knowledge to make doubly clear how different his new religion was to be considered from that of ancient Judaism. He reminded his listeners that no one sews a piece of unshrunken cloth over a hole in an old garment. When the garment is washed, the patch will shrink and pull out the weakened threads of the old garment, thus leaving an even larger hole than before. Equally common was the knowledge of the second illustration that he employed to make this point, namely, that no one puts new wine into old wineskins since new wine in its fermenting stage would be likely to burst the old skins.

The new gospel that Christ is preaching, if it were simply meant to modify ancient Judaism, would work like a piece of unshrunken cloth when applied to an old garment. It would do harm to this ancient religion or, even worse, like pouring new wine into old wineskins, it would ruin both the old and the new religions. The "good news" cannot be assimilated into the old ceremonial forms of Judaism with the latter's emphasis upon fasting, for example, and its lack of clarity about the hereafter, without endangering the existence of both. They were frankly incompatible.

The principal difficulty suggested by the above text is the implication that Christ was willing for Judaism to be preserved, that the religion of the "good news" need not completely replace it. Luke not only implies this interpretation, he confirms it: "And no one after drinking old wine desires new for he says, 'The old is good'" (5:39). Despite all of Christ's teaching and its attractiveness, there will be some who will continue to prefer traditional Judaism to the new covenant, and it almost appears as if Christ was willing to accept such a decision on their part.

Still, most commentators rule out this interpretation. They prefer to describe Luke's statement as ironical, that the evangelist was simply lamenting the fact that most men are inclined to cling to established beliefs and customs and to prefer these to the new and revolutionary. It has also been suggested that Matthew, in recording (editing?) Christ's words, permitted his interest in completing the literary parallelism—"and so both are preserved"—to introduce an interpretation that was never intended.

Christ spoke these words immediately following his discussion with the disciples of John about the failure of his own disciples to fast. (See above, p. 40.) For this reason, some commentators say it is possible to construe Christ's warning against patching tears with new cloth and putting new wine into old wineskins as aimed at John's disciples rather than at the Jews in general. John's disciples insisted on remaining loyal to the Baptist even though the "good news" of the kingdom of God was being preached.

* * *

CHRIST limited his preaching to Judea and Galilee, to Hebrews who shared many of his own views concerning God. Matthew has him instructing his apostles to observe the same limitation, that is, to preach only to Jews.

The passage reads:

> The names of the twelve apostles are these: first, Simon, who is called Peter. . . . These twelve Jesus sent out, charging them, "Go nowhere among the Gentiles, and enter no town of the Samaritans, but go rather to the lost sheep of the house of Israel. And preach as you go, saying, 'The kingdom of heaven is at hand'" (Matthew 10:2-7).

In the art of preaching and making converts to the new order, the disciples at this point in their association with Christ had just completed their apprenticeship. They were now ready to go out on their own and spread the "good news." Still they remained tyros faced with a difficult task, and it was for this reason that Christ warned them to limit their first efforts to the Jews, to God's Chosen People, to those who had either grown careless in the worship of the one true God or who had abandoned that faith. They were not to go among the Gentiles, and these included the Samaritans who professed a kind of polytheism. These last the disciples would find infinitely more difficult to convert. Christ may also have feared that the Samaritans would find the ways of his Jewish disciples offensive.

For the more difficult problem regarding Christ's own attitude toward the Samaritans (Gentiles), see below, p. 66.

*   *   *

WHAT marks men and women of deep faith is their un-wavering trust in God. Whatever may happen, they are convinced God is there, looking on as it were, fully aware of what is transpiring. This text in Matthew has helped establish that kind of unquestioning faith and trust.

The passage reads:

"And do not fear those who kill the body but cannot kill the soul; rather fear him who can destroy both soul and body in hell. Are not two sparrows sold for a penny? And not one of them will fall to the ground without your Father's will. But even the hairs of your head are all numbered. Fear not, therefore; you are of more value than many sparrows" (Matthew 10:28-31).

Christ is reassuring his disciples that they are not to be frightened of the Pharisees and of others who would find their teaching offensive and take steps to silence them. To drive home a point, Christ delighted in using figurative language. His reference to the hairs of one's head and the Father's concern about sparrows is an excellent example. In this he wished to emphasize in a way his disciples would never forget God's unceasing care for all men and his complete love for each individual, particularly for those who did his will. Yet he does not promise his disciples that they will escape suffering, even death. He later warned them that their enemies "will deliver you up to tribulation and put you to death; and you will be hated by all nations" (Matthew 24:9).

* * *

ONE of the most perplexing texts in Matthew, one that continues to divide biblical scholars in their analyses, tells of the impact Christ's teaching will have on families. The text has Christ, the "Prince of Peace," stating quite frankly that he has come to sow bitterness among members of a family, to cause dissension and conflict.

The text reads:

> "So every one who acknowleges me before men, I also will acknowledge before my Father who is in heaven; but whoever denies me before men, I also will deny before my Father who is in heaven. Do not think that I have come to bring peace on earth; I have not come to bring peace, but a sword. For I have come to set a man against his father, and a daughter against her mother, and a daughter-in-law against her mother-in-law; and a man's foes will be those of his own household. He who loves father or mother more than me is not worthy of me; and he who loves son or daughter more than me is not worthy of me; and he who does not take his cross and follow me is not worthy of me. He who finds his life will lose it, and he who loses his life for my sake will find it" (Matthew 10:32-39).

These words sound sharply contradictory to the promise sung out by the angels when announcing to the shepherds the birth of the new-born Christ: "Glory to God in the highest, and on earth peace among men with whom he is pleased!" (Luke 2:14). Christ is speaking here as no prince of peace but as a serious teacher about to send his disciples out to preach. He is warning them that they will not only encounter persecution but that their message will cause families to split asunder. "Brother will deliver up brother to death, and the father his child, and children will rise against parents and have them put to death'' (Matthew 10:21). (See also Mark 13:12.)

Commentators generally view this admonition as a warning that Christ chose to overstate in order to lend it greater force. It should be weighed against the softer reminder contained in verses 37-38 of this same chapter, namely, "He who loves father or mother more than me is not worthy of me; and he who loves son or daughter more than me is not worthy of me; and he who does not take his cross and follow me is not worthy of me." (Luke 14:26, is more severe. See below, p. 127.)

Commentators agree that Christ did not come to sow strife among members of a family even though his message might have that consequence. Once men and women have accepted and applied his gospel, there would come an end to strife, not only within the family itself but among peoples as well. Yet anyone who would become his follower must be prepared to do so at the risk of antagonizing relatives and friends.

One wonders why Christ chose to express this thought in such grim language. His words surely do not fit the first Christian communities. These had their unbelieving neighbors marveling at how much these Christians loved one another. Despite Christ's dour prediction, instances of a father turning his son over to be executed and of a son his father, are hard, if not impossible, to find. Is Christ here suggesting a situation that seldom arose or, as some commentators suggest, is he actually speaking from experience? Had he encountered such hostility among his own kinsmen (brethren) that he felt obliged to warn his disciples that they should expect the same result? If so, Christ's observations that "a man's foes will be those of his own household" holds particular pertinency. (See below, p. 97.)

*   *   *

ON no human individual did Christ bestow greater praise than on John the Baptist. "Truly, I say to you . . . there has risen no one greater than John the Baptist." Then he proceeded to qualify, actually negate that statement with "yet he who is least in the kingdom of heaven is greater than he."

The passage reads:

As they went away, Jesus began to speak to the crowds concerning John: "What did you go out into the wilderness to behold? A reed shaken by the wind? Why then did you go out? To see a man clothed in soft raiment? Behold, those who wear soft raiment are in kings' houses. Why then did you go out? To see a prophet? Yes, I tell you, and more than a prophet. This is he of whom it is written, 'Behold, I send my messenger before thy face, who shall prepare thy way before thee.' Truly I say to you, among those born of women there has risen no one greater than John the Baptist; yet he who is least in the kingdom of heaven is greater than he" (Matthew 11:7-11).

A literal interpretation of this text will lead many astray. Christ was not concerned with satisfying any possible curiosity his listeners might harbor regarding the virtues of John the Baptist, whether he might rank as number one among all men in our Lord's estimation, or number two, or six. Christ's purpose was to affirm how far superior the spiritual character and capacity of the lowest soul in his kingdom was above that of even so sublime a person as John. A literal understanding of Christ's statement would leave John not only superior to Mary but to Christ himself who was also born of woman.

True, John was the greatest of the prophets and the last in the line of eminent men who had preached the coming of the Messiah. As a child of grace, John shared, of course, in the promise of the New Testament, as would all holy people of the Old Testament. Yet he had not been destined to take an active part in the kingdom that he had prophesied would come. From the nature of his preaching, he belonged to the old dispensation, the era of preparation, of which he was the last and the supreme product. In terms of spiritual privileges, grace, and knowledge, even the humblest members of the kingdom were superior to him. He remained a servant; they were children, sons of Christ.

No doubt Christ's praise of John pleased the Baptist's disciples and helped set at rest any question they might have had concerning the Lord's esteem for their master. Christ's thought is, nonetheless, quite clear: It is better to be a member of the kingdom than to herald its coming.

*　*　*

CHRISTIANS have learned that God can forgive all sins, even the blackest, and the divine attribute that men and women find most appealing is his mercy: God is all-merciful. Yet here Matthew has Christ warning his listeners, the Pharisees in particular but all people in general, that sins against the Holy Spirit will never be forgiven, "either in this age or in the age to come."

The passage reads:

Then a blind and dumb demoniac was brought to him, and he healed him, so that the dumb man spoke and saw. And all the people were amazed, and said, "Can this be the Son of David?" But when the Pharisees heard it they said, "It is only by Be-elzebul, the prince of demons, that this man casts out demons." Knowing their thoughts, he said to them, "Every kingdom divided against itself is laid waste, and no city or house divided against itself will stand; and if Satan casts out Satan, he is divided against himself; how then will his kingdom stand? And if I cast out demons by Be-elzebul, by whom do your sons cast them out? Therefore they shall be your judges. But if it is by the Spirit of God that I cast out demons, then the kingdom of God has come upon you. Or how can one enter a strong man's house and plunder his goods, unless he first binds the strong man? Then indeed he may plunder his house. He who is not with me is against me, and he who does not gather with me scatters. Therefore I tell you, every sin and blasphemy will be forgiven men, but the blasphemy against the Spirit will not be forgiven. And whoever says a word against the Son of man will be forgiven; but whoever speaks against the Holy Spirit will not be forgiven, either in this age or in the age to come'' (Matthew 12:22-32).

Many theologians have found this passage difficult inasmuch as it assumes God cannot forgive all sins. What Christ probably had in mind here is the proud person who stubbornly resisted the truth, a characterization that would appear to fit the Pharisees. They were willing to admit his miraculous powers, but they attributed these to the cooperation of the devil. Mark makes this clear. After saying essentially what Matthew did about the unforgivable nature of such sins, he writes of these Pharisees: "For they had said, 'He has an unclean spirit'" (3:30).

Christ's reference to himself as the Son of man and his assurance that a sin against him may therefore be forgiven serve to distinguish between those men who did not recognize his divine nature or the working of the Spirit in him, and the Pharisees who knew this. His warning may, accordingly, have been meant specifically for the Pharisees and perhaps for no one else, although to deliberately ascribe the unmistakable workings of God to the power of the evil spirit suggests so reprobate an attitude as to deprive that person of the divine mercy by simply denying its existence. St. Jerome writes that he who clearly perceives the works of God but out of envy ascribes them to the devil, closes the door to forgiveness.

Since Christ had not preached about the Holy Spirit as a member of the Trinity, the reference to the Spirit is believed not to refer to the Third Person but to divine grace in general. Any willful, free, and persisting denial of the working of the divine spirit, particularly in the case of miracles when their effects were manifest, was a sin against the Spirit.

Some theologians refuse to accept the unforgivable nature of any sins and view such a position as a strictly human limitation on the divine mercy. They interpret Christ's words as intended purely as a warning to the Pharisees who were fast approaching moral disaster in their hatred of him. These theologians make their appeal to the passage in the Acts (26:14) that describes Paul's conversion: "And when we had all fallen to the ground, I heard a voice saying to me in the Hebrew language, 'Saul, Saul, why do you persecute me? It hurts you to kick against the goads.'" Still Paul, as opposed to the Pharisees, was no hypocrite.

* * *

PROBABLY the most controversial passage in Matthew, to the layperson surely the most disturbing, is this one where the evangelist speaks of Christ's brothers.

The passage reads:

> While he was still speaking to the people, behold, his mother and his brothers stood outside, asking to speak to him. But he replied to the man who told him, "Who is my mother, and who are my brothers?" And stretching out his hand toward his disciples, he said, "Here are my mother and my brothers! For whoever does the will of my Father in heaven is my brother, and sister, and mother" (Matthew 12:46-50).

The only Christians who take the above reference to the brothers of Christ in stride are those who believe Mary bore children after she had Jesus. For those Christians, Roman Catholics in particular, who believe Mary remained a virgin throughout her life, the text creates real difficulty. The parallel passage in Mark (3:31-35) aggravates their problem by adding sisters to the brothers who wish to see Jesus. (Matthew 13:56 and Mark 6:3, also speak of sisters.) Other passages in the gospels, as well as in the Acts and epistles, make reference to Christ's brothers. (See Luke 8:19-21; John 2:12; 7:3,5,10; Acts 1:14; 12:17; 15:13; 21:18; 1 Corinthians 9:5; 15:7; Galatians 1:19.)

Although the question of Mary's perpetual virginity has evoked much learned discussion, major disagreement persists. Part of the inability of biblical scholars to agree on the relationship between these "brothers" and Christ stems from doubt as to whom the evangelists meant when they used the word "brothers." The term might refer to kinsmen, cousins for instance, as well as to blood brothers.

St. Jerome pressed this argument in a tract that he wrote in 383 A.D. against a certain Helvidius who had claimed these "brothers" were Christ's own blood brothers, therefore the sons of Mary. Jerome insisted the evangelists spoke of "brothers" since the ancient Hebrew and Aramaic languages lacked a word for cousins. This deficiency had forced the scholars who translated the Old Testament from these Semitic languages into the so-called Septuagint (third century B.C.) to employ the Greek word for brothers when the text actually read kinsmen. In so doing, Jerome argued, they established a usage that the evangelists adopted.

The passage in John (19:25) that tells of the women who gathered at the foot of the cross on Calvary might throw decisive light on the problem if only the evangelist had been more precise in his language. John reads: "But standing by the cross of Jesus were his mother, and his mother's sister, Mary the wife of Clopas, and Mary Magdalene." Biblical scholars argue, first, over the number of women at the cross. Does John list three or four? Then they disagree over the identity of the women introduced. Mary Magdalene occasions no difficulty, neither does Mary, Christ's mother. But who was his mother's sister and who was Mary, the wife of Clopas? Are they one and the same person? Mark (15:40-41) lists by name Mary Magdalene, Salome, and Mary, the mother of James the Younger and Joses (Joset). Matthew (27:55-56) mentions Mary Magdalene, Mary the mother of James and Joseph, also the mother of the sons of Zebedee (James and John). Luke (23:49) speaks only of "women who had followed him from Galilee." Not only do scholars disagree over the exact identity of several of these women, but one or the other exegete even denies the historicity of John's account about the women actually being at the cross since the three older synoptic gospels keep them at a distance.

Had the medieval church not appealed to a tradition of Mary's perpetual virginity that it insisted reached back to the very beginnings of Christianity, the controversy would probably have subsided long ago, indeed, may never have risen. During the first three centuries of the Christian era, that virginity appears to have been asssumed rather than preached. Because only scattered references to Mary's perpetual virginity remain from this early period, one could conclude that this question was considered of little moment. The earliest work to extol Christian virginity was from the pen of St. Methodius of Olympus who died in 311, and it was only after monasticism had made virginity the prerequisite to a truly spiritual life that Mary's perpetual virginity took on real importance. Once this happened, stalwart champions of that view pressed forward, notably St. Jerome (d. 420) and St. Ambrose (d. 397), who composed tracts on the subject of virginity and exalted Mary as the exemplar of that virtue. Their immense influence assured acceptance of Mary's perpetual virginity as a matter of faith.

What was the position of the few church fathers who adverted to the subject of Mary's perpetual virginity before the time of Ambrose and Jerome? It appears they favored that virginity although none judged the matter of such significance as to warrant extended discussion. Most important and influential of these early church fathers was Origen (d. 254?). In his commentary on this passage in Matthew (12:46-50) he writes that there were some men who believed, on the basis of the *Gospel according to Peter*, that the brothers of Christ mentioned by the evangelist were the sons of Joseph by an earlier wife, accordingly, not Mary's children. Origen went on to say that apologists for that view maintained this in order "to preserve the honor of Mary in virginity to the end," and he seems to have concurred with their judgment.

It is true that the *Gospel according to Peter* to which Origen referred, together with several other writings of this early period that touched upon Mary's perpetual virginity, have been judged apocryphal. Still, from the fact that contemporaries as learned as Origen accepted them as authentic, one might assume the belief in Mary's perpetual virginity must have been almost universal.

Who then were the brothers spoken of by the evangelist? Origen probably supposed they were sons of Joseph by an earlier wife, and such was the view of Gregory of Nyssa (d. 386), Hilary of Poitiers (d. 367?), and Eusebius of Caesarea (d. 339?), to mention several of the more important fathers of a later period. Jerome says they were Christ's cousins. Ambrose did not bother to discuss the matter.

Several circumstances favored the view that they were sons of Joseph by an earlier wife. Leaving these "brothers" to be only half-brothers would explain why Christ preferred to entrust his mother to his beloved apostle John, possibly his cousin, rather than to half-brothers who had never accepted him. (See John 7:5, and below, p. 151.) It would also explain the friction, if not hostility, that may have existed between Jesus and his "brothers" (see below, pp. 97-98), a situation more common among half-brothers than blood brothers. Then the reference to Jesus as the son of Mary (Mark 6:3) rather than the son of Joseph (scholars assume Joseph was already dead), an identification that in biblical times could carry a slur of bastardy, would have lost its offensiveness. That the medieval church recognized the "brothers" as Christ's cousins was due to its sanctifying Jerome's judgment as definitive.

One last point: It is difficult to say Christ's "brothers" were really his disciples in view of the clear distinction John (2:12; 7:2-5) draws between them. (See also Mark 3: 20-21, 31-35.)

* * *

ASK a Christian what he knows best about the gospels, and he will usually say the parables. Parables like those of the Good Samaritan, the Good Shepherd, and the Prodigal Son have a way of living on, even in the memories of people who have turned their backs on Christianity. Their memory lingers on, not only because the stories are themselves interesting, but because of the moral lessons they teach. Here is a passage in Matthew, however, that leads one to wonder whether Christ always intended his parables to hold a moral lesson, to assist him in his work of preaching the "good news."

The passage reads:

Then the disciples came and said to him, "Why do you speak to them in parables?" And he answered them, "To you it has been given to know the secrets of the kingdom of heaven, but to them it has not been given. For to him who has will more be given, and he will have abundance; but from him who has not, even what he has will be taken away. This is why I speak to them in parables, because seeing they do not see, and hearing they do not hear, nor do they understand. With them indeed is fulfilled the prophecy of Isaiah which says: 'You shall indeed hear but never understand, and you shall indeed see but never perceive. For this people's heart has grown dull, and their ears are heavy of hearing, and their eyes they have closed, lest they should perceive with their eyes, and hear with their ears, and understand with their heart, and turn for me to heal them, But blessed are your eyes, for they see, and your ears, for they hear" (Matthew 13:10-16).

It was immediately after Christ had concluded telling the

"great crowds" the parable of the sower who went out to sow seed—"A sower went out to sow. And as he sowed, some seeds fell along the path, and the birds came and devoured them"—that the disciples put this question to him, "Why do you speak to them in parables?"

The sense of the above passage becomes even more difficult to penetrate when considered alongside verse 34 that follows. This reads: "All this Jesus said to the crowds in parables; indeed he said nothing to them without a parable." (See also Mark 4:10-12, and Luke 8:9-10.) The question is this then, why did Christ speak to the crowds at all in parables if these were presented in such a manner as to confuse, or remain meaningless to them?

To propose, first, a positive explanation of the meaning of the passage: Christ must have interpolated parables with some regularity into his preaching, the sense of which, even though pertinent, might be above the heads of the majority of his listeners. He may have done this to break the monotony of his discourse in the hope of regaining the attention of those whose minds had wandered. Some would consider the parable a good story in itself without appreciating its relevancy. The parable would also give his listeners something to reflect upon after they had returned to their homes. Such stories would remain in their memory after the instructions which they were intended to illustrate had long been forgotten and do some belated good in bringing these lessons back to mind. The recollection of these parables might indeed arouse those who were inclined to be dull and mentally lazy, might haunt the minds of the stubborn until they reformed.

That some of Christ's parables passed over the heads of the people who listened to him may be assumed from the nature of his disciples' complaint, "Why do you speak to them in parables?" Still, a number of Christ's parables required little or no explanation, like that about the unjust servant who was forgiven a large debt only to turn around and imprison one of his debtors who owed him very little (Matthew 18:23-35). Even a less simple parable like that of the Prodigal Son would announce a moral that was self-evident—a father should always be willing to forgive a contrite son—while containing other lessons that were not so evident. In this instance, the Pharisees might recognize themselves in the person of the older brother who objected to his father's forgiving the younger son. (See below, p. 130.) Or consider the parable of the Good Samaritan. Again, the immediate moral is so manifest as to require no explanation, but the Pharisees would perceive in the failure of the priest and Levite to succor the wounded traveler as a criticism of the Old Law that they sanctified. (See below, p. 120.)

Christ must have made a practice of meeting with his disciples after having preached to the multitude in order to clarify for them things he had said, parables, in particular, to make sure they understood what he intended. He could not afford to burden his audience with extended explanations for fear of losing their attention. The suggestion of other implications that his words might carry could await the later appearance of his disciples whom he would meantime have instructed more fully in the matter. That these disciples must still have wondered what the gist of his parables might have been, even after his explanations, is suggested by the relief they expressed at the Last Supper when Christ spoke to them directly, and not in parables: their comment, "Ah, now you are speaking plainly, not in any figure!" (John 16:29).

Now for the negative aspect of Christ's words, where he

says he was speaking to them in parables because, although having the power to see, they did not see and having the power to hear they did not hear nor understand. Mark says the same in blunter language: "lest they should turn again, and be forgiven" (4:12).

Christ must have been speaking of those people who did not come to listen to him in a spiritually receptive mood. This would include not only the Pharisees but many more, for he repeats the prophet's lament that "this people's heart has grown dull." In any event, only those who were willing to believe would derive any benefit from what he said, "For to him who has will more be given, and he will have abundance; but from him who has not, even what he has will be taken away."

Those individuals among his listeners, including his disciples, who had either already accepted him or were willing to hear him with open minds, they would receive yet more. The obstinate among his audience, the Pharisees in particular, would be deprived of what little they had. For in not receiving the kingdom of God they would be losing everything. Only those who accepted Christ would profit from what he said, only those would be able to understand what he was saying.

Still on the subject of parables—Matthew in chapter 13 appears to be reassuring the reader that Christ always intended his parables to edify his audience, to instruct them in the principles of the "good news," even though all their possible interpretations might escape them for the time.

The passage reads:

All this Jesus said to the crowds in parables; indeed he said nothing to them without a parable. This was to fulfill what was spoken by the prophet: "I will open my mouth in parables, I will utter what has been hidden since the foundation of the world'' (Matthew 13:34-35).

In a parallel passage Mark (4:33-34) has somewhat more to say. He writes: ''With many such parables he spoke the word to them, as they were able to hear it; he did not speak to them without a parable, but privately to his own disciples he explained everything.''

These passages from Matthew and Mark show Christ as regularly gracing his sermons with parables. He did this for a variety of reasons: to illustrate with an exemplar-story some point that he attempted to make in his preaching; to break the monotony of his discourse, as any speaker does with the help of anecdotes and stories; to leave his audience with an interesting story to mull over, one that they would be likely to remember long after they had forgotten the instructions which they were intended to illustrate, but whose recollection would then remind them of those lessons.

One may conclude from these passages that Christ did not expect his audience to comprehend the meaning of every one of his parables, surely not the different levels of application the more complex of these parables might invite. The point of the parable of the unjust servant would be readily comprehensible, but not that of the laborers in the vineyard or the several interpretations to which the parable of the Good Samaritan lends itself. After the crowd had dispersed and Christ was alone with his disciples, he would explain any parable whose meaning was not self-evident and suggest further applications for those parables that might hold more than one meaning. (See above, p. 59.)

* * *

A familiar maxim that a variety of situations is apt to bring to mind reached back to Christ's "A prophet is not without honor except in his own country and in his own house." It seems the people of Nazareth, his own home, even his own relatives, did not believe in Christ. This is the startling fact as Matthew describes it.

The passage reads:

> And when Jesus had finished these parables, he went away from there, and coming to his own country he taught them in their synagogue, so that they were astonished, and said, "Where did this man get this wisdom and these mighty works? Is not this the carpenter's son? Is not his mother called Mary? And are not his brothers James and Joseph and Simon and Judas? And are not all his sisters with us? Where then did this man get all this?" And they took offense at him. But Jesus said to them, "A prophet is not without honor except in his own country and in his own house." And he did not do many mighty works there, because of their unbelief (Matthew 13:53-58).

Substantially the same description of this incident appears in Mark (6:3) although that evangelist has the people wondering, "Is not this the carpenter, the son of Mary?" This is the sole reference in the gospels to Christ's being a carpenter, although it is traditional to assume that he was.

Luke's account varies in several interesting details. First, he has the people who listened to Christ being greatly impressed at his words: "And all spoke well of him, and wondered at the gracious words which proceeded out of his mouth." Not only was the initial response of the people more friendly than Matthew leads us to believe, but Luke has them asking, "Is not this Joseph's son?" This almost suggests that Joseph was still alive, which is not what is generally believed. However friendly the first reaction of the people of Christ's neighborhood to his preaching, it shortly turned hostile and they forced him to leave their community (Luke 4:22-30).

For a consideration of the question whether Christ had brothers and sisters, see above, p. 54. There are other references in the gospels to members of Christ's family, kinsmen if not brothers, who did not accept him. See John 7:5, and below, p. 151.

* * *

RARELY do the evangelists have Jesus using harsh words except with the Pharisees. Here is one of those rare instances. Jesus apparently spoke ungraciously to a woman who had begged his help for her sick daughter.

The passage reads:

> And Jesus went away from there and withdrew to the district of Tyre and Sidon. And behold, a Canaanite woman from that region came out and cried, "Have mercy on me, O Lord, Son of David: my daughter is severely possessed by a demon." But he did not answer her a word. And his disciples came and begged him, saying, "Send her away, for she is crying after us." He answered, "I was sent only to the lost sheep of the house of Israel." But she came and knelt before him, saying, "Lord, help me." And he answered, "It is not fair to take the children's bread and throw it to the dogs." She said, "Yes, Lord, yet even the dogs eat the crumbs that fall from their masters' table." Then Jesus answered her, "O woman, great is your faith! Be it done for you as you desire." And her daughter was healed instantly (Matthew 15:21-28).

Expositors have long puzzled over two aspects of this passage: first, the rough language Christ employed in speaking to the distraught woman; second, the geographical or national limits he placed upon his mission. On this last point, commentators generally assume that Christ did not feel his mission extended to any people beyond his fellow Jews. He was later quite precise in setting the same restriction on the activity of his disciples. (See above, p. 44.) In their case, they were short of both knowledge and experience, at least initially; in his case, he was short of time. Later he did spend two days preaching to the Samaritans but only upon their urgent request. (See John 4:40.) The nationality of the woman remains in doubt since the geographical setting of the incident is not clear. She may have been a Phoenician woman, not a Jewess.

The simile of the dog sounds offensive to our ears. The original Greek speaks of little dogs or whelps, which reduces somewhat the sting in Christ's words. Then, too, Christ may have had a smile on his face when he spoke these words, which would make it easier for the woman to give the "clever" reply that she made. There remains, too, the difficulty of translating into a modern language the exact sense of an idiomatic expression or possibly even a proverb in use two thousand years ago. Mark (7:24-30) gives the same incident, but nothing appears in either Luke or John.

* * *

FEW of Christ's firm promises have occasioned more controversy than the following. Christ assured his audience that some of them will still be alive when he entered into his kingdom.

The passage reads:

"Truly, I say to you, there are some standing here who will not taste death before they see the Son of man coming in his kingdom" (Matthew 16:28).

What Christ meant by his kingdom is not clear. He told Pilate that his kingdom was not of this world (John 18:36). Earlier, in answer to a question put to him by the Pharisees as to when the kingdom of God would come, he told them that the kingdom "of God is not coming with signs to be observed; nor will they say, 'Lo, here it is!', or 'There!' for behold, the kingdom of God is in the midst of you" (Luke 17:20-21). And he charged the Pharisees with blocking the coming of that kingdom.

It is possible that Christ believed his gospel, his church, his kingdom, would spread more rapidly than it did, although he regularly cautioned his disciples not to waste their time seeking to learn the exact time of future events. Just as regularly, however, did he warn them to be prepared at all times. Like the prophets of the Old Testament, Jesus saw what the future would bring, but he may have miscalculated the speed with which it was coming. On his own admission, he did not know the time the world would come to its end, "but the Father only" (Matthew 24:36).

Some early commentators believed the reference to the kingdom was to Pentecost. The apostle John may have understood it to have already arrived since in his day the Jewish nation had been scattered and the Temple destroyed, while the gospel was being preached in much of the Mediterranean world. Many of the first Christians were convinced the kingdom referred to Christ's return, to his second coming, which they expected momentarily. Stephen, just before being stoned to death by his enemies, exclaimed, "Behold, I see the heavens opened, and the Son of man standing at the right hand of God" (Acts 7:56). For Stephen, God's kingdom had indeed arrived. For Peter, Christ's transfiguration may have constituted the coming of his kingdom. (See 2 Peter 1:16-18.)

* * *

ON several occasions Christ showed himself impatient, even hostile, toward the Pharisees. Here in Matthew, he evinces a measure of irritation and impatience with his disciples.

The passage reads:

And when they came to the crowd, a man came up to him and kneeling before him said, "Lord, have mercy on my son, for he is an epileptic and he suffers terribly; for often he falls into the fire, and often into the water. And I brought him to your disciples, and they could not heal him." And Jesus answered, "O faithless and perverse generation, how long am I to be with you? How long am I to bear with you? Bring him here to me." And Jesus rebuked him, and the demon came out of him, and the boy was cured instantly. Then the disciples came to Jesus privately and said, "Why could we not cast it out?" He said to them, "Because of your little faith. For truly, I say to you, if you have faith as a grain of mustard seed, you will say to this mountain, 'Move from here to there,' and it will move; and nothing will be impossible to you. [But this kind never comes out except by prayer and fasting.]"* (Matthew 17:14–21). *The bracketed passage appears as verse 21 in some ancient manuscripts.

The parallel passages in Mark (9:17–29) and Luke (9:38–42) offer no clue as to whom Christ addressed his impatient words. He surely did not intend them for the father of the sick boy since it was his faith in Christ's healing powers that had prompted him to bring his son to be cured. Neither may the crowd be judged the target of Christ's sharp language since it had assembled largely in awe of Christ's fame as a preacher and a wonder-worker. This leaves only the disciples, and Matthew appears to suggest that it was they who drew Christ's ire. After Christ had expelled the demon and cured the boy, Matthew has the disciples asking Jesus, in private, why they had been unable to do this, and his answer to them was, "Because of your little faith." Mark (9:29) is less critical. To their question why they failed to drive out the devil, Jesus explained, "This kind cannot be driven out by anything but prayer."

Two explanations offer themselves to account for Christ's seeming irritation. Time after time Christ showed his knowledge of the Old Testament especially in his arguments with the Pharisees. Here he might well have been giving voice to the same complaint God made to Moses over the refusal of the Hebrews to believe in him after all he had done for them. (See Numbers 14:11). In Deuteronomy (32:5) Israel, because of its lack of faith, is described as a "perverse and crooked generation." John the Baptist used similarly harsh words—"brood of vipers" (Luke 3:7)—when condemning them for their lack of faith. One may assume that given similar circumstances, that sort of harsh language would not have been deemed out of place, even from the lips of Jesus.

This suggests a second explanation for the unusual harshness of Christ's language, namely, that the evangelists were simply placing in Christ's mouth the kind of expression which such a lack of faith might have provoked. One may ask whether Christ ever spoke those precise words. They were written down no earlier than thirty years after his death on the strength of the testimony made by men who could scarcely have been present when Christ presumably spoke them and who in all probability could neither read nor write and whose memories may not have been any more dependable than our own. We live in an age that can hear and record every last word an important person might say on a special occasion. Nothing approaching this in the way of accurate recording was possible in antiquity. It was also accepted practice at that time for most writers, even for historians who were held to tell the truth, to enliven their accounts with quotations, even entire speeches, that they had made out of whole cloth.

* * *

OF the three theological virtues, Christ placed greatest emphasis on faith, a faith that can move mountains!

The passage reads:

> "For truly, I say to you, if you have faith as a grain of mustard seed, you will say to this mountain, 'Move from here to there,' and it will move; and nothing will be impossible to you" (Matthew 17:20).

All three synoptic evangelists record this statement. (See Mark 11:22-23, and Luke 17:6.) Matthew repeats it in a slightly different, though more emphatic manner: "And Jesus answered them, 'Truly, I say to you, if you have faith and never doubt, you will not only do what has been done to the fig tree (see below, p. 84) but even if you say to this mountain, "Be taken up and cast into the sea," it will be done'" (21:21). Luke writes: "If you had faith as a grain of mustard seed, you could say to this sycamore tree, 'Be rooted up, and be planted in the sea,' and it would obey you." This statement strikes the reader as even more preposterous than Matthew's.

These statements are perhaps the most extreme of the hyperbolical expressions that Christ made use of, and he employed a good many. His hope was to make a deep impression on his listeners, and no doubt he succeeded. Those few souls who might attempt to apply Christ's assurance literally were in for disappointment. The individual who expects God to hear his prayer, must have faith, and a person with faith will not ask for anything trivial or absurd, such as having God cause a mountain to move out of the way. Some theologians will maintain that the person with faith will never ask for material blessings. What examples the evangelists offer of Christ's own prayers, those in Gethsemane, for instance, and on the cross, have him qualifying his plea with, "Not my will but thine be done."

What Christ hoped to accomplish by speaking in this figurative language was to emphasize in the strongest possible manner what truly great achievements faith in God can work. Within a few centuries of Christ's death, this faith had converted the pagan Roman empire, and during the early centuries of the Middle Ages it proved itself the principal agent in civilizing the peoples who had destroyed that empire.

*   *   *

DID Christ qualify his instruction that his followers must always be ready to forgive any who offended them? The following passage suggests he did.

> "If your brother sins against you, go and tell him his fault, between you and him alone. If he listens to you, you have gained your brother. But if he does not listen, take one or two others along with you, that every word may be confirmed by the evidence of two or three witnesses. If he refuses to listen to them, tell it to the church; and if he refuses to listen even to the church, let him be to you as a Gentile and a tax collector" (Matthew 18:15-17).

The harshness of Christ's instruction, that the erring, unrepentant brother be treated as a Gentile or tax collector, may disturb many Christians, and this for two reasons: first, it seems to imply Christ's approval of the antipathy Jews had for non-Jews and for publicans; second, it is inconsistent with the picture the gospels give of Christ as constantly urging forgiveness: e.g., Christ telling Peter to forgive an offending brother, not seven times, "but seventy times seven" (Matthew 18:22).

The problem invites an easy solution if one may assume Christ is speaking, not of a blood brother, but of a "brother" as a member of the Christian community. In all probability, that is what he was doing. The fault of the erring brother was, accordingly, not of a personal nature as against another individual, as would be that of striking him a blow on the face. It was rather the kind of conduct Christians judged incompatible with their faith and principles, as, for example, that of a married man living with a woman other than his wife. This sort of behavior the

Christian community could not tolerate in any "brother." Should he refuse to correct his way of living, he must be excluded from the community of Christians, be treated as a Gentile and tax collector, since his continued presence there would threaten the stability and integrity of their community.

On the other hand, while the Christian community should expel such an erring "brother" from their society, they must continue to associate with him socially and show him the love and sympathy which they owed him as a fellow creature of God. They must continue to be on friendly terms with him just as Christ was with publicans and sinners: "Now the tax collectors and sinners were all drawing near to hear him. And the Pharisees and the scribes murmured, saying, 'This man receives sinners and eats with them'" (Luke 15:1-2).

While the textual reading, "If your brother sins against you" may suggest an offense of a personal nature, Christ's own attitude toward Gentiles and publicans, as reflected in the text above, would appear to rule out such an interpretation. The phrase *against you* is, furthermore, absent from several of the oldest and most authoritative manuscripts of Matthew's gospel.

It should be noted that Christ is here counseling the procedure that the law of Moses prescribed in instances of this kind, first, that of speaking privately to the erring brother (Leviticus 19:17), next, should this prove ineffective, of bringing along one or more others to serve as witnesses (Deuteronomy 19:15). The last resort, that of finally excluding the individual from the Christian community, was already adopted by Paul (see 1 Corinthians 5:9) in the case of fornicators. Actually the entire episode appears to be more in keeping with the method which the early church adopted in handling the problem of recalcitrant members than with the attitude Christ had for nonconformists.

* * *

CHRISTIANS, also many non-Christians, are acquainted with Christ's warning about the difficulty the rich will have in gaining heaven. Matthew adds a twist to that warning that invites profound consideration.

The passage reads:

> And Jesus said to his disciples, "Truly, I say to you, it will be hard for a rich man to enter the kingdom of heaven. Again I tell you, it is easier for a camel to go through the eye of a needle than for a rich man to enter the kingdom of God." When the disciples heard this they were greatly astonished, saying, "Who then can be saved?" But Jesus looked at them and said to them, "With men this is impossible, but with God all things are possible" (Matthew 19:23-26).

The setting for this well-known warning that Christ leveled at the wealthy was the decision of a rich young man not to join the company of his disciples since to do this he had first to dispose of his possessions. The young man had asked Jesus what he must do to gain eternal life, and Christ had told him to keep the commandments. When the young man assured Christ that he had been observing the commandments all his life but wondered what more he might have to do, Jesus had explained that if he wished indeed to be perfect, he must "go, sell what you possess and give to the poor . . . and come, follow me" (19:21).

What Christ was condemning here was not so much wealth in itself as the avid accumulation of material goods as an end in itself, in a measure far beyond one's needs, and with a selfish indifference to the needs of the poor. Since men of moderate means, even poor people, can harbor the same preoccupation with material goods, the warning that Christ applied here to the wealthy would also pertain to them. Mark's language suggests this broader application. He writes, "How hard it will be for those who have riches to enter the kingdom of God!" (10:23). Christ counted several men of considerable wealth among his friends, e.g., Matthew, Joseph of Arimathea, and Zacchaeus. Zacchaeus was clearly not of the wealthy sort whom Christ condemned since he gave half of his substance to the poor (Luke 19:8).

Christ's use of the figurative camel passing through the eye of a needle is an excellent example of his unique ability at hyperbolical speech. The expression appears to have been a popular proverb among Jews at the time. It had the meaning of attempting the impossible. By joining his warning about wealth with this hyperbole Christ was certain to leave a deep impression with his listeners. His words so shocked his disciples that they asked, with a measure of anxiety, "Who then can be saved?"

All men require God's grace to be saved, and God is willing to bestow his help wherever it is wanted. Since the wealthy person, because of his material blessings, may be more inclined to subordinate the spiritual to the temporal, he may be less concerned about seeking God's grace, and receive less as a consequence, for which reason Christ may have intended his warning principally for the rich.

The astonishment of the disciples at Christ's warning raises the possibility that, poor as they were, they may have feared that his words were also meant for them. The nature of their question, "Who then can be saved?" supports this interpretation. In all probability Christ was directing his warning about wealth to a much larger audience than simply the rich, and the real concern of his disciples would seem to bear this out. Such an interpretation would also better suit Christ's statement, "With men this is impossible, but with God all things are possible."

* * *

THE parable about the workers in the vineyard, all of whom received the same pay, is among the best-known of Christ's stories, and one of the most misunderstood.

The passage reads:

"For the kingdom of heaven is like a householder who went out early in the morning to hire laborers for his vineyard. After agreeing with the laborers for a denarius a day, he sent them into his vineyard. And going out about the third hour he saw others standing idle in the market place; and to them he said, 'You go into the vineyard too, and whatever is right I will give you.' So they went. Going out again about the sixth hour and the ninth hour, he did the same. And about the eleventh hour he went out and found others standing; and he said to them, 'Why do you stand here idle all day?' They said to him, 'Because no one has hired us.' He said to them, 'You go into the vineyard too.' And when evening came, the owner of the vineyard said to his steward, 'Call the laborers and pay them their wages, beginning with the last, up to the first.' And when those hired about the eleventh hour came, each of them received a denarius. Now when the first came, they thought they would receive more; but each of them also received a denarius. And on receiving it they grumbled at the householder, saying, 'These last worked only one hour, and you have made them equal to us who have borne the burden of the day and the scorching heat.' But he replied to one of them, 'Friend, I am doing you no wrong; did you not agree with me for a denarius? Take what belongs to you, and go; I choose to give to this last as I give to you. Am I not allowed to do what I choose with what belongs to me? Or do you begrudge my generosity?' So the last will be first, and the first last'' (Matthew 20:1-16).

This remains one of the most controversial of Christ's parables. At first glance it appears to violate a fundamental principle of justice, surely a modern application of this, namely, that pay for hourly work should be commensurate with the time put in. Even Christ's listeners who lived long before men began to speak seriously of the rights of the laborer must have puzzled more over the apparent injustice done those who had worked a full day rather than over the "break" the generosity of the landlord had given the latecomers. Christ must actually have hoped that would be their reaction since he makes a point of emphasizing the fact that those who had labored longest had also "borne the burden of the day and the scorching heat."

The usual approach to explaining this parable is to equate the value of the denarius with that of eternal life or heaven. The value of this latter is absolute and unrestricted: it can neither be increased nor diminished. It is the same for all. Next, the value of eternal life or of heaven is so tremendous it bears no conceivable relationship to the amount of effort any person might expend to achieve it, whatever his motivation and industry. It remains, accordingly, essentially a gift, not a wage. God is ready to give this gift to all, to the person who has served him his entire life as well as the laggard who for a variety of reasons has delayed his conversion until the last moment. The thief on the cross entered paradise a few moments after his conversion. (See Luke 23:43.)

Several other aspects of the parable invite consideration. One is the selfishness of the laborers who had put in a full day's work and who resented the generosity of the landlord in dealing so graciously with those who had done little. Implied here is Christ's criticism of those who would pass judgment on the manner God sees fit to bestow the blessing of eternal life. It should be noted that the laborers received their pay in reverse order so that those who had worked longest would be sure to see how well those fared who had put in but little time. Had they received their wage first, they would have taken their pay and gone home.

The parable carries a warning against the danger of self-righteousness, against the comfortable notion that a person can establish a claim upon God by living what the individual feels to be a good and worthy life. On the other hand, the parable holds out God's promise to deal more than generously with all, even with those who have done little to merit his good will. The parable may contain, finally, a reference to the Jews, who for more than a thousand years under the Old Covenant had been working for eternal life. They will receive no more in the end than the Gentiles who would only now be coming to believe.

The cryptic statement that follows this passage in Matthew, that the last shall be first and the first last, refers to those individuals whom the world judges to be first and most important but who will fare no better than the most humble. They will receive no more than those whom the world judges least deserving.

*   *   *

FIGS were a popular fruit in Palestine, almost a staple in that country. Matthew has Christ cursing a fig tree for failing to have fruit, thus using his power to cause the tree to wither. Why did he do this?

The passage reads:

> In the morning, as he was returning to the city, he was hungry. And seeing a fig tree by the wayside he went to it, and found nothing on it but leaves only. And he said to it, "May no fruit ever come from you again!" And the fig tree withered at once. When the disciples saw it they marveled, saying, "How did the fig tree wither at once?" And Jesus answered them, "Truly, I say to you, if you have faith and never doubt, you will not only do what has been done to the fig tree, but even if you say to this mountain, 'Be taken up and cast into the sea,' it will be done. And whatever you ask in prayer, you will receive, if you have faith" (Matthew 21:18-22).

This remains among the more perplexing stories in the gospels. As one commentator has it, it is easy to understand why Luke omitted it! For one thing, it is the one instance where Christ is shown exercising his miraculous powers in a destructive fashion. Then Mark (11:13) makes the situation worse by stating quite frankly that it was not the season for figs. Should one, therefore, charge Christ with possessing less knowledge than the ordinary native about the proper season for figs and, beyond that, with displaying a fit of childish petulancy in cursing the tree when he found it barren?

About the matter whether it was the season for figs, as Mark states, it was not. Matthew corroborates this. He has the incident taking place in the early spring of the Passover season, whereas figs in Palestine do not ripen until June. It is true that fig trees may put forth an early crop which is edible although not eaten because of the fruit's disagreeable taste. It is also possible that some of the natives, then as well as now, were willing to sample the young green fruit before it ripened. This might have been the case with Jesus since he was hungry. Still, even if Christ could have expected to find something to eat on the tree, this did not excuse his cursing the tree when he found none.

Most commentators give little time to the question whether figs were in season or not. They assign the incident a wholly symbolic interpretation, namely, that Christ was here formally turning his back on Judaism, that he was looking forward to the imminent fall of Jerusalem and the destruction of the Temple. In both Matthew and Mark the cursing of the tree took place immediately following Christ's triumphant entry into Jerusalem. They tell next about the fig tree, followed in Mark with Christ cleansing the Temple of buyers and sellers, in Matthew with a bitter exchange of words between Christ and the chief priests, which sharp confrontation Christ terminates with the solemn warning: "Therefore I tell you, the kingdom of God will be taken away from you and given to a nation producing the fruits of it" (21:43).

These commentators judge the fig tree to symbolize Judaism and the Temple. As Christ approached the tree from a distance, it appeared to be healthy and full of leaves. When he drew near and gave it a closer look, he discovered only leaves, no fruit, for which reason he cursed it. With this curse he was symbolically thrusting Judaism and the Temple aside. Their fate was to be that of the fig tree.

It has been suggested that Matthew presents a sort of dramatized cast to the episode of the fig tree as this is

described in Luke (13:6-9). Luke tells how the owner of a
fig tree had tired of the tree's lack of productivity and had
instructed the vine-dresser to cut it down. The latter had
objected and begged the owner to give him some time during which he would cultivate and manure the tree. "And if
it bears fruit next year, well and good; but if not, you can
cut it down." Christ in cursing the fig tree had presumably
run out of patience with Judaism and had decided to be
done with it.

Christ may have cursed the fig tree simply to demonstrate to his disciples both his divine power as well as the
power of faith. The verses that follow suggest this interpretation. Matthew writes: "When the disciples saw it they
marveled, saying, 'How did the fig tree wither at once?'
And Jesus answered, 'Truly, I say to you, if you have faith
and never doubt, you will not only do what has been done
to the fig tree, but even if you say to this mountain, 'Be
taken up and cast into the sea' it will be done.' " (20:22).

Note might be made of the discrepancy between the accounts in Matthew and Mark regarding the withering of
the tree. In Matthew the tree withered immediately; in
Mark it did not. (See Mark 11:20-21.)

*   *   *

SOON after telling of the episode about the fig tree Matthew has Christ again issuing that sober warning, "Many are called but few chosen."

The passage reads:

And again Jesus spoke to them in parables, saying, "The kingdom of heaven may be compared to a king who gave a marriage feast for his son, and sent his servants to call those who were invited to the marriage feast; but they would not come. Again he sent other servants, saying, 'Tell those who are invited, Behold, I have made ready my dinner, my oxen and my fat calves are killed, and everything is ready; come to the marriage feast.' But they made light of it and went off, one to his farm, another to his business, while the rest seized his servants, treated them shamefully, and killed them. The king was angry, and he sent his troops and destroyed those murderers and burned their city. Then he said to his servants, 'The wedding is ready, but those invited were not worthy. Go therefore to the thoroughfares, and invite to the marriage feast as many as you find.' And those servants went out into the streets and gathered all whom they found, both bad and good; so the wedding hall was filled with guests.

"But when the king came in to look at the guests, he saw there a man who had no wedding garment; and he said to him, 'Friend, how did you get in here without a wedding garment?' And he was speechless. Then the king said to the attendants, 'Bind him hand and foot, and cast him into the outer darkness; there men will weep and gnash their teeth.' For many are called, but few are chosen" (Matthew 22:1-14).

Christ concludes this parable about the wedding feast with the admonition that many are called but few chosen in order to make it clear God has invited all to follow him. Many refuse his invitation outright, they are unconcerned and ignore his message. Others are hostile, seize his messengers, and put them to death. These messengers are the prophets of the Old Testament and John the Baptist of the New. Some of these men fared poorly at the hands of the Jews, and so will Christ who here assumes the role of a prophet regarding his own end.

There are theologians who insist that God, in theory at least, is free to condemn all men to hell. There are other theologians, perhaps the same ones, who feel God's mercy is so all-embracing that very few if any will be denied eternal life. It is a curious fact that in antiquity, and that would include Christ's period, most people believed in a life after death but one that would consist of a dismal existence except for a favored few. Today when most people have but a hazy view of eternal life, the general assumption is that if there is indeed a life after death, this life will prove to be a reasonably comfortable one and one which all will share alike.

The man without the wedding garment represents the person who answers God's call but makes no effort to show by his behavior that he has indeed responded. The wedding garment symbolizes a willingness to accept God's invitation and the intention to do what is necessary to be worthy of that invitation. Some commentators go further; Roman Catholic theologians in particular interpret the wedding feast as symbolizing the Eucharist, the man without a wedding garment, a person not in the state of grace.

The terms *many* and *few* are not to be understood as

measures of mathematical precision. Christ employed them simply to add emphasis to his warning that the believer should not abuse God's grace.

* * *

A GOOD illustration of the danger of taking Christ's words literally appears here in the Lord's admonition, "Call no man your father."

The passage reads:

> Then said Jesus to the crowds and to his disciples, "The scribes and the Pharisees sit on Moses' seat; so practice and observe whatever they tell you, but not what they do; for they preach, but do not practice. They bind heavy burdens, hard to bear, and lay them on men's shoulders; but they themselves will not move them with their finger. They do all their deeds to be seen by men; for they make their phylacteries broad and their fringes long, and they love the place of honor at feasts and the best seats in the synagogues, and salutations in the market places, and being called rabbi by men. But you are not to be called rabbi, for you have one teacher, and you are all brethren. And call no man your father on earth, for you have one Father, who is in heaven. Neither be called masters, for you have one master, the Christ. He who is greatest among you shall be your servant; whoever exalts himself will be humbled, and whoever humbles himself will be exalted" (Matthew 23:1–12).

The words with which Christ concludes this discourse reveal the point of his instruction, namely, that the proud shall be humbled and the humble honored. Christ's injunction to call no one teacher (rabbi) or father is not to be taken literally, rather in the implied sense that no one, regardless of his station, should ever forget that he remains very much a human being, a mere creature of the Almighty. All good, wisdom, and virtue come from the one and only God, who is rabbi, teacher, and father.

* * *

TOWARD the end of his life, Christ had some disquieting and puzzling predictions to make about the end of the world, so puzzling in fact, that biblical scholars have not been entirely successful in explaining them.

The passage reads:

> "Immediately after the tribulation of those days the sun will be darkened, and the moon will not give its light, and the stars will fall from heaven, and the powers of the heavens will be shaken; then will appear the sign of the Son of man in heaven, and then all the tribes of the earth will mourn, and they will see the Son of man coming on the clouds of heaven with power and great glory; and he will send out his angels with a loud trumpet call, and they will gather his elect from the four winds, from one end of heaven to the other.

> "From the fig tree learn its lesson: as soon as its branch becomes tender and puts forth its leaves, you know that summer is near. So also, when you see all these things, you know that he is near, at the very gates. Truly, I say to you, this generation will not pass away till all these things take place. Heaven and earth will pass away, but my words will not pass away.

> "But of that day and hour no one knows, not even the angels of heaven, nor the Son, but the Father only" (Matthew 24:29-36.

This remains one of the most controversial passages in the gospels. The source of the difficulty stems from two of Christ's statements, first, that all these things, namely, the destruction of Jerusalem, the end of the world, and the second coming of Christ (*parousia*) will take place before his generation had come to an end, and, second, that concerning the end of the world and the second coming, no one knew the precise time, not even he himself, but only the Father.

If by all these things Christ included the destruction of Jerusalem, the end of the world, and his *parousia*, then he was clearly mistaken when he affirmed that all would take place within the lifetime of many of the people in his audience. It is possible that Christ did not reckon a generation to cover thirty or forty years, although his giving a generation a longer span would only leave him correct with regard to the destruction of Jerusalem (70 A.D.).

A possible solution to the problem of how Christ could be so mistaken may be found in the apocalyptic language he liked to use. He speaks, for example, of heaven and earth passing away. To his listeners this simply meant the same as never, or that there existed a greater likelihood of their passing away than that of his prophecy concerning the future's not being fulfilled. People of biblical times accepted this sort of eschatological language in a way our pragmatic society finds impossible. Surely few people who heard him tell of the lilies of the field that never worked yet were taken care of by God (Matthew 6:29) quit their jobs forthwith. Neither would they have held Christ to an exact application of his prediction regarding the end of the world, although Paul and many of his fellow Christians believed his second coming was imminent. (See 1 Thessalonians 4:13-18; 1 Corinthians 1:7-8; 4:5.) Christ employed this colorful language simply to add greater force to the warning that follows in verse 42, namely, "Watch therefore, for you do not know on what day your Lord is coming." It should be noted, furthermore, that Matthew may be combining in one discourse a number of predictions which Christ actually delivered on different occasions.

Christ's statement that only the Father knew the precise day and hour of these future events would appear to diminish his divine nature. It was for this reason that St. Ambrose dismissed the passage as an Arian interpolation. And the position of Ambrose pretty well stamped biblical thinking until recent years.

It is true that the phrase, "nor the Son," is missing from a number of the important manuscripts of Matthew's gospels, and it does not appear in Luke, but it does in Mark (13:32). Many exegetes today accept the historicity of the statement and find it consistent with the picture of Christ's human nature as suggested in John 5:19, Hebrews 2:17 and 4:15. They argue that Christ, though the Son of God, so emptied himself of divinity (Philippians 2:6-8) through his incarnation that as the Son of man he received divine powers from the Father only to the extent that these were necessary for the fulfillment of his mission. The knowledge as to when the world would come to an end or the time of his second coming, presumably did not fall into the category of knowledge essential to that mission.

* * *

DID Christ succumb or come near succumbing to despair during his agony on the cross? Matthew's account leaves us wondering.

The passage reads:

Now from the sixth hour there was darkness over all the land until the ninth hour. And about the ninth hour Jesus cried with a loud voice, "Eli, Eli, lama sabachthani?" that is, "My God, my God, why hast thou forsaken me?" (Matthew 27:45-46).

Some commentators trace this terrifying cry of Jesus to his human nature. Although both human and divine, here at the moment of death and greatly weakened by both physical and mental suffering, Christ found himself on the threshold of despair. Christ had confessed to his low emotional state the night before, in the garden of Gethsemane when he told Peter, James, and John, "My soul is very sorrowful, even to death; remain here, and watch with me" (26:38). Christ may have permitted himself to sink to the deepest level of human misery and suffering in order to afford reassurance to others caught in a similar state, that God is still with those who persist in their faith.

Since the words of Christ are those that open Psalm 22, it has been suggested that Christ was here simply reciting that part of the psalm. He may indeed have recited the psalm in its entirety, with only this portion of it being heard and recorded. And the psalm itself, although it begins on this despairing note, constitutes in fact a prayer of confidence in God and of trust in his mercy. Thus Paul wrote in his Letter to the Hebrews (5:7): "In the days of his flesh, Jesus offered up prayers and supplications, with loud cries and tears, to him who was able to save him from death, and he was heard for his godly fear."

THE GOSPEL ACCORDING TO MARK

And a leper came to him beseeching him, and kneeling said to him, "If you will, you can make me clean." Moved with pity, he stretched out his hand and touched him, and said to him, "I will; be clean." And immediately the leprosy left him, and he was made clean. And he sternly charged him, and sent him away at once, and said to him, "See that you say nothing to any one; but go, show yourself to the priest, and offer for your cleansing what Moses commanded, for a proof to the people" (Mark 1:40-44). See above, p. 32.

*   *   *

Now John's disciples and the Pharisees were fasting; and people came and said to him, "Why do John's disciples and the disciples of the Pharisees fast, but your disciples do not fast?" And Jesus said to them, "Can the wedding guests fast while the bridegroom is with them? As long as they have the bridegroom with them, they cannot fast. The days will come, when the bridegroom is taken away from them, and then they will fast in that day" (Mark 2:18-20). See above, p. 40.

*   *   *

"No one sews a piece of unshrunk cloth on an old garment; if he does, the patch tears away from it, the new from the old, and a worse tear is made. And no one puts new wine into old wineskins; if he does, the wine will burst the skins, and the wine is lost, and so are the skins;

but new wine is for fresh skins'' (Mark 2:21-22). See above, p. 42.

*   *   *

ONE of the most disturbing passages in the gospels is Mark's statement that the "family" of Christ came to bring him back to Nazareth since they were convinced he was out of his mind.

The passage reads:

And when his family heard it, they went out to seize him, for people were saying, "He is beside himself" (Mark 3:21).

Matthew who follows Mark's gospel during these sections omits these lines, and there is no echo of them in either Luke or John. Exactly to whom Mark is referring when he writes "his family" is a matter of some controversy. It has been suggested that they were friends, neighbors, or cousins who had heard alarming stories about the strange things Jesus had been preaching, stories that had undoubtedly grown more disquieting in their retelling. These concerned people had come to take Jesus back with them to Nazareth, perhaps as much to protect him from violence as out of concern over his mental health. Some commentators maintain that the "family" referred to were Christ's own brothers—they assume he had several—who did not approve of what he was preaching and had come to take him back to his home. The position of Mary, Christ's mother, in this matter is not mentioned, although some commentators believe she must have agreed with the "family" since she would otherwise not have come along (verse 31, and see above, p. 54).

Those scholars who maintain it was Christ's own brothers who had come to take him back home find support for their interpretation in several other passages in the gospels. On one occasion Christ spoke of a prophet as being without honor in his own country (Matthew 13:57, Luke 4:24, and see above, p. 64). On another occasion he warned his listeners that his preaching would tear families apart, turn father against son and daughter against mother, which may suggest dissension among members of his own family, (See above, p. 46). Finally, toward the close of this passage in Mark (31-35), the evangelist tells how Christ's mother and brothers had come from Nazareth and had reached the outside circle of his listeners, when they made it known they were anxious to speak to him. See above, p. 54.

* * *

"Truly, I say to you, all sins will be forgiven the sons of men, and whatever blasphemies they utter; but whoever blasphemes against the Holy Spirit never has forgiveness, but is guilty of an eternal sin"—for they had said, "He has an unclean spirit" (Mark 3:28-30). See above, p. 51.

* * *

And his mother and his brothers came; and standing outside they sent to him and called him. And a crowd was sitting about him and they said to him, "Your mother and your brothers are outside, asking for you." And he replied, "Who are my mother and my brothers?" And looking around on those who sat about him, he said, "Here are my mother and my brothers! Whoever does the will of God is my brother, and sister, and mother" (Mark 3:31-35). See above, p. 54.

* * *

And he said to them, "Take heed what you hear; the measure you give will be the measure you get, and still more will be given you. For to him who has will more be given; and from him who has not, even what he has will be taken away" (Mark 4:24-25). See above, p. 59.

* * *

They came to the other side of the sea, to the country of the Gerasenes. And when he had come out of the boat, there met him out of the tombs a man with an unclean spirit, who lived among the tombs; and no one could bind him any more, even with a chain; for he had often been bound with fetters and chains, but the chains he wrenched apart, and the fetters he broke in pieces; and no one had the strength to subdue him. Night and day among the tombs and on the mountains he was always crying out, and bruising himself with stones. And when he saw Jesus from afar, he ran and worshipped him; and crying out with a loud voice, he said, "What have you to do with me, Jesus, Son of the Most High God? I adjure you by God, do not torment me." For he had said to him, "Come out of the man, you unclean spirit!" And Jesus asked him, "What is your name?" He replied, "My name is Legion; for we are many." And he begged him eagerly not to send them out of the country. Now a great herd of swine was feeding there on the hillside; and they begged him, "Send us to the swine, let us enter them." So he gave them leave. And the unclean spirits came out, and entered the swine; and the herd, numbering about two thousand, rushed down the steep bank into the sea, and were drowned in the sea (Mark 5:1-13). See above, p. 38.

*   *   *

AN interesting illustration of the individual ways the evangelists record the same incident appears in the story of the woman suffering from a hemorrhage. Matthew gives but a few lines and so also Luke. Luke's reticence has suggested the facetious explanation that, being a physician himself, he did not relish recording his profession's inadequacy. The fullest account appears in Mark.

The passage reads:

> And there was a woman who had a flow of blood for twelve years, and who had suffered much under many physicians, and had spent all that she had, and was no better but rather grew worse. She had heard the reports about Jesus, and came up behind him in the crowd and touched his garment. For she said, "If I touch even his garment, I shall be made well." And immediately the hemorrhage ceased; and she felt in her body that she was healed of her disease. And Jesus, perceiving in himself that power had gone forth from him, immediately turned about in the crowd, and said, "Who touched my garments?" And his disciples said to him, "You see the crowd pressing around you, and yet you say, 'Who touched me?'" And he looked around to see who had done it. But the woman, knowing what had been done to her, came in fear and trembling and fell down before him, and told him the whole truth. And he said to her, "Daughter, your faith has made you well; go in peace, and be healed of your disease" (Mark 5:25-34). (See Matthew 9:20-22, and Luke 8:43-48.)

The woman's malady, probably a menstrual disorder as Pope Gregory the Great intimated, made her ceremonially unclean and would also leave others unclean who came in contact with her. (See Leviticus 15:27.) Not only modesty, therefore, but fear of publicly admitting her uncleanness may explain the covert manner she went about touching Christ's garment. And so quietly did she accomplish this that Christ did not notice her touch, although he did sense that power had gone out from him. So in order that the miraculous power of the Father receive recognition, he immediately asked who had touched him.

There appears no question that Jesus did not know who had touched him nor the reason why the person had done so. From the somewhat critical question of his disciples who wondered why he should be asking such a question in view of the large crowd milling about him, one must conclude that Christ realized it was the one who touched him, who had faith in being cured, that was responsible for the power leaving him. To do honor to the Father, therefore, and to demonstrate his own role in the work of the Father, the miracle done that person must be made manifest.

Two observations come to mind, first, that Christ merits no criticism for forcing the poor woman to reveal her embarrassing condition since he did not know who had touched him nor the nature of her problem. The second observation is the more significant, namely, that the Father had apparently worked a miracle without the direct intervention of Jesus except that it had been worked through him. See above, p. 93.

* * *

He went away from there and came to his own country; and his disciples followed him. And on the sabbath he began to teach in the synagogue; and many who heard him were astonished, saying, "Where did this man get all this? What is the wisdom given to him? What mighty works are wrought by his hands! Is not this the carpenter, the son of Mary and brother of James and Joses and Judas and Simon, and are not his sisters here with us?" And they took offense at him. And Jesus said to them, "A prophet is not without honor, except in his own country, and among his own kin, and in his own house." And he could do no mighty work there, except that he laid his hands upon a few sick people and healed them. And he marveled because of their unbelief (Mark 6:1-6). See above, p. 64.

* * *

And from there he arose and went away to the region of Tyre and Sidon. And he entered a house, and would not have any one know it; yet he could not be hid. But immediately a woman, whose little daughter was possessed by an unclean spirit, heard of him, and came and fell down at his feet. Now the woman was a Greek, a Syrophoenician by birth. And she begged him to cast the demon out of her daughter. And he said to her, "Let the children first be fed, for it is not right to take the children's bread and throw it to the dogs." But she answered him, "Yes, Lord; yet even the dogs under the table eat the children's crumbs." And he said to her, "For this saying you may go your way; the demon has left your daughter." And she went home, and found the child lying in bed, and the demon gone (Mark 7:24-30). See above, p. 66.

* * *

THERE is extensive duplication in the three synoptic gospels, those of Matthew, Mark and Luke. Mark writes of one incident, not discussed elsewhere, and it is unique. It tells of Christ working a miracle in stages.

The passage reads:

> And they came to Bethsaida. And some people brought to him a blind man, and begged him to touch him. And he took the blind man by the hand, and led him out of the village; and when he had spit on his eyes and laid his hands upon him, he asked him, "Do you see anything?" And he looked up and said, "I see men; but they look like trees, walking." Then again he laid his hands upon his eyes; and he looked intently and was restored, and saw everything clearly. And he sent him away to his home, saying, "Do not even enter the village" (Mark 8:22-26).

This is the only instance the gospels record what might be described as a case of "gradual healing," and Mark is alone in introducing it. The use of saliva for medical purposes was common in antiquity since it was believed to possess curative powers. It remained part of the baptismal rite in the Roman Catholic Church until a few years ago.

Christ may have employed a "gradual" process in curing the man of his blindness in order to suggest the tardy working of the man's faith. The man may not have been completely convinced of Christ's ability to heal him. The narrative leaves the impression that he had not come on his own initiative. His friends brought him, and he did not fall on his knees and beg to be cured of his blindness as had others who sought Christ's help.

That Christ instructed the man not to return to his village seems strange since that was where his friends and relatives probably lived. (See above, p. 32, for other instances when Christ ordered men whom he had cured to be silent about the miracles worked in their behalf.)

* * *

And when they came to the disciples, they saw a great crowd about them, and scribes arguing with them. And immediately all the crowd, when they saw him, were greatly amazed, and ran up to him and greeted him. And he asked them, "What are you discussing with them?" And one of the crowd answered him, "Teacher, I brought my son to you, for he has a dumb spirit; and whenever it seizes him, it dashes him down; and he foams and grinds his teeth and becomes rigid; and I asked your disciples to cast it out, and they were not able." And he answered them, "O faithless generation, how long am I to be with you? How long am I to bear with you? Bring him to me." And they brought the boy to him; and when the spirit saw him, immediately it convulsed the boy, and he fell on the ground and rolled about, foaming at the mouth. And Jesus asked his father, "How long has he had this?" And he said, "From childhood. And it has often cast him into the fire and into the water, to destroy him; but if you can do anything, have pity on us and help us." And Jesus said to him, "If you can! All things are possible to him who believes." Immediately the father of the child cried out and said, "I believe; help my unbelief!" And when Jesus saw that a crowd came running together, he rebuked the unclean spirit, saying to it, "You dumb and deaf spirit, I command you, come out of him, and never enter him again.'' And after crying out and convulsing him terribly, it came out, and the boy was like a corpse; so that most of them said, ''He is dead.'' But Jesus took him by the hand and lifted him up, and he arose. And when he had entered the house, his disciples asked him privately, ''Why could we not cast it out?'' And he said to them, ''This kind cannot be driven out by anything but prayer'' (Mark 9:14–29). See above, p. 70.

* * *

''And if your hand causes you to sin, cut it off; it is better for you to enter life maimed than with two hands to go to hell, to the unquenchable fire. And if your foot causes you to sin, cut it off; it is better for you to enter life lame than with two feet to be thrown into hell. And if your eye causes you to sin, pluck it out; it is better for you to enter the kingdom of God with one eye than with two eyes to be thrown into hell, where their worm does not die, and the fire is not quenched'' (Mark 9:43-48). See above, p. 19.

* * *

THE language of the gospels has Christ speaking on occasion in less than gracious words. Mark records one such occasion.

The passage reads:

> And as he was setting out on his journey, a man ran up and knelt before him, and asked him, "Good Teacher, what must I do to inherit eternal life?" And Jesus said to him, "Why do you call me good? No one is good but God alone. You know the commandments. . . ." (Mark 10:17-18).

Christ's abrupt reply to the young man's seemingly polite question has received several explanations. Commentators suggest that Christ may have detected a note of flattery in the man's salutation, perhaps of glibness as in the modern practice of hailing another as "Doc" or "Captain." The usual explanation is that Christ took this opportunity to emphasize the point that all goodness had its source in God. Only God is good and everything good about man and in what he does can only reflect that goodness. Since Christ, after some questioning, found the young man to be wholly sincere—Jesus looked steadily at him and loved him—suggests that he had never doubted the young man's good faith. (See below, p. 137 for a similar incident recorded in Luke. See also above, p. 90.)

* * *

And Jesus looked around and said to his disciples, "How hard it will be for those who have riches to enter the kingdom of God!" And the disciples were amazed at his words. But Jesus said to them again, "Children, how hard it is to enter the kingdom of God! It is easier for a camel to go through the eye of a needle than for a rich man to enter the kingdom of God." And they were exceedingly astonished and said to him, "Then who can be saved?" Jesus looked at them and said, "With men it is impossible, but not with God; for all things are possible with God" (Mark 10:23-27). See above, p. 78.

*   *   *

On the following day, when they came from Bethany, he was hungry. And seeing in the distance a fig tree in leaf, he went to see if he could find anything on it. When he came to it, he found nothing but leaves, for it was not the season for figs. And he said to it, "May no one ever eat fruit from you again." And his disciples heard it. . . .

As they passed by in the morning, they saw the fig tree withered away to its roots. And Peter remembered and said to him, "Master, look! The fig tree which you cursed has withered." And Jesus answered them, "Have faith in God. Truly, I say to you, whoever says to this mountain, 'Be taken up and cast into the sea,' and does not doubt in his heart, but believes that what he says will come to pass, it will be done for him" (Mark 11:12-14, 20-23). See above, p. 84.

*   *   *

"From the fig tree learn its lesson: as soon as its branch becomes tender and puts forth its leaves, you know that summer is near. So also, when you see these things taking place, you know that it is near, at the very gates. Truly, I say to you, this generation will not pass away before all these things take place. Heaven and earth will pass away, but my words will not pass away. But of that day or that hour no one knows, not even the angels in heaven, nor the Son, but only the Father" (Mark 13: 28-32). See above, p. 91.

*   *   *

And at the ninth hour Jesus cried with a loud voice, "Eloi, Eloi, lama sabach-thani?" which means, "My God, my God, why hast thou forsaken me?" (Mark 15: 34). See above, p. 94.

*   *   *

THE GOSPEL ACCORDING TO LUKE

THE evangelists and their Christian contemporaries understood the meaning of the words and expressions recorded in the gospels better than we in this modern world. We have difficulty, for example, with Luke's description of the presentation of the child Jesus in the Temple.

The passage reads:

> And his father and his mother marveled at what was said about him; and Simeon blessed them and said to Mary his mother, "Behold, this child is set for the fall and rising of many in Israel, and for a sign that is spoken against (and a sword will pierce through your own soul also), that thoughts out of many hearts may be revealed" (Luke 2:33-35).

Commentators have found this is a difficult passage. A suggested interpretation of the words, "this child is set for the fall and rising of many in Israel," is that while God has sent his son to save all men, some will accept him, others will reject him. His coming will, accordingly, serve to separate the righteous from the wicked. Christ will stand as a sign of contradiction. To some he will prove to be a pillar of strength, a cornerstone; others will simply turn their backs on him. Still, all will be obliged to take a stand, either for or against him.

The words that Simeon addressed to Mary, "a sword will pierce through your own soul," has received conflicting interpretations. Some scholars believe it to be a reference to Christ's death, which tragic event would pierce Mary's heart. Other commentators consider the reference is to the sufferings (sorrows) that Christ would experience because of the sins of Israel, as foretold him in Isaiah 53.

* * *

LUKE follows up his account of the presentation of the child Jesus in the Temple with another puzzling story, that of Christ being lost to his parents for three days.

The passage reads:

> After three days they found him in the temple, sitting among the teachers, listening to them and asking them questions; and all who heard him were amazed at his understanding and his answers. And when they saw him they were astonished; and his mother said to him, "Son, why have you treated us so? Behold, your father and I have been looking for you anxiously." And he said to them, "How is it that you sought me? Did you not know that I must be in my Father's house?" And they did not understand the saying which he spoke to them. And he went down with them and came to Nazareth, and was obedient to them; and his mother kept all these things in her heart. And Jesus increased in wisdom and in stature, and in favor with God and man (Luke 2:46-52).

Not only did Mary puzzle over this incident but modern commentators as well. Mary's perplexity suggests she had never fully comprehended the implications of the role she had accepted when she announced to Gabriel her willingness to be the mother of God's son. That the nature of this commitment remained something of a mystery to her is intimated by Luke when he describes the visit of the shepherds to the stable to see the Christ child. Luke writes: "But Mary kept all these things, pondering them in her heart" (2:19). Then again on the occasion of Mary's purification, when Simeon spoke to Joseph and Mary about their child (see above, p. 110), Luke comments: "His father and his mother marveled at what was said about him"

(2:33). This was the first time, at any rate, that Christ, now twelve years of age, informed his mother that as the Son of God he had a special role in life, and his words indicate surprise that his parents were not aware of that fact.

That Christ's anxious parents may have spent relatively little time in searching for him—in all probability they only missed him the evening of the first day, then hurried back to Jerusalem the second day, and discovered him on the third—may reassure those who would reproach Christ for his apparent lack of consideration. Finally, when the evangelist speaks of Christ's growing in wisdom, this is generally understood to refer to the measure of his experiential knowledge. As the son of a human mother, the knowledge that reflected that human nature would have developed and increased much like that of other boys. It would only have been over a period of time, for instance, that he acquired the skills of a carpenter.

There are commentators who doubt the historicity of this incident.

* * *

Jesus, when he began his ministry, was about thirty years of age, being the son (as was supposed) of Joseph, the son of Heli, the son of Matthat, the son of Levi . . . the son of Enos, the son of Seth, the son of Adam, the son of God (Luke 3:23-24, 38). See above, p. 9.

* * *

While he was in one of the cities, there came a man full of leprosy; and when he saw Jesus, he fell on his face and besought him, "Lord, if you will, you can make me clean." And he stretched out his hand, and touched him, saying, "I will; be clean." And immediately the leprosy left him. And he charged him to tell no one; but "go and show yourself to the priest, and make an offering for your cleansing, as Moses commanded, for a proof to the people." But so much the more the report went abroad concerning him; and great multitudes gathered to hear and to be healed of their infirmities. But he withdrew to the wilderness and prayed (Luke 5: 12-16). See above, p. 32.

* * *

And they said to him, "The disciples of John fast often and offer prayers, and so do the disciples of the Pharisees, but yours eat and drink." And Jesus said to them, "Can you make wedding guests fast while the bridegroom is with them? The days will come, when the bridegroom is taken away from them, and then they will fast in those days" (Luke 5:33-35). See above, p. 40.

* * *

He told them a parable also: "No one tears a piece from a new garment and puts it upon an old garment; if he does, he will tear the new, and the piece from the new will not match the old. And no one puts new wine into old wineskins; if he does, the new wine will burst the skins and it will be spilled, and the skins will be destroyed. But new wine must be put into fresh wine-skins. And no one after drinking old wine desires new: for he says, 'The old is good'" (Luke 5:36-39). See above, p. 42.

* * *

"But I say to you that hear, Love your enemies, do good to those who hate you, bless those who curse you, pray for those who abuse you. To him who strikes you on the cheek, offer the other also and from him who takes away your coat do not withhold even your shirt. Give to every one who begs from you; and of him who takes away your goods do not ask them again (Luke 6:27-30). See above, p. 23.

* * *

CHRIST knew he was not the kind of Messiah many Jews expected. Even good men would be disappointed, other men like John the Baptist, not sure. So John sent two of his disciples to ask Christ, "Are you he who is to come, or shall we look for another?" (Luke 7:20).

The passage reads:

> And he answered them, "Go and tell John what you have seen and heard: the blind receive their sight, the lame walk, lepers are cleansed, and the deaf hear, the dead are raised up, the poor have good news preached to them. And blessed is he who takes no offense at me" (Luke 7:22-23).

Jesus was bound to be a disappointment to the many Jews who had expected him to free them from Roman rule. Besides these there were others, notably the Pharisees, who were willing to admit that Christ did work wonders, yet refused to accept these miracles as proof he was the Messiah. To do so demanded greater courage, humility, and willingness to repent than many possessed. That John the Baptist wondered whether Christ was the Messiah comes as a surprise. He must have heard of the miracles that Christ had worked but still remained unconvinced. And it was John who baptized Christ when, according to Matthew (3:17), the heavens were opened and a voice from heaven announced, "This is my beloved Son, with whom I am well pleased." That even John held back makes it easier to understand why most Jews did not accept Christ as the Messiah.

*   *   *

"I tell you, among those born of women none is greater than John yet he who is least in the kingdom of God is greater than he" (Luke 7:28). See above, p. 49.

*   *   *

And when his disciples asked him what this parable meant, he said, "To you it has been given to know the secrets of the kingdom of God; but for others they are in parables, so that seeing they may not see, and hearing they may not understand" (Luke 8:9-10). See above, p. 59.

*   *   *

"For nothing is hid that shall not be made manifest, nor anything secret that shall not be known and come to light. Take heed then how you hear; for to him who has will more be given, and from him who has not, even what he thinks that he has will be taken away" (Luke 8:17-18). See above, p. 59.

*   *   *

Then his mother and his brothers came to him, but they could not reach him for the crowd. And he was told, "Your mother and your brothers are standing outside, desiring to see you." But he said to them, "My mother and my brothers are those who hear the word of God and do it." (Luke 8:19-21). See above, p. 54.

*   *   *

Then they arrived at the country of the Gerasenes, which is opposite Galilee. And as he stepped out on land, there met him a man from the city who had demons; for a long time he had worn no clothes, and he lived not in a house but among the tombs. When he saw Jesus, he cried out and fell down before him, and said with a loud voice, "What have you to do with me, Jesus, Son of the Most High God? I beseech you, do not torment me." For he had commanded the unclean spirit to come out of the man. (For many a time it had seized him; he was kept under guard, and bound with chains and fetters, but he broke the bonds and was driven by the demon into the desert.) Jesus then asked him, "What is your name?" And he said, "Legion"; for many demons had entered him. And they begged him not to command them to depart into the abyss. Now a large herd of swine was feeding there on the hillside; and they begged him to let them enter these. So he gave them leave. Then the demons came out of the man and entered the swine, and the herd rushed down the steep bank into the lake and were drowned (Luke 8:26-33). See above, p. 38.

*   *   *

As he went, the people pressed round him. And a woman who had had a flow of blood for twelve years and could not be healed by any one, came up behind him, and touched the fringe of his garment and immediately her flow of blood ceased. And Jesus said, "Who was it that touched me?" When all denied it, Peter said, "Master, the multitudes surround you and press upon you!" But Jesus said, "Some one touched me; for I perceive that power has gone forth from me."

And when the woman saw that she was not hidden, she came trembling, and falling down before him declared in the presence of all the people why she had touched him, and how she had been immediately healed. And he said to her, "Daughter, your faith has made you well; go in peace" (Luke 8:42-48). See above, p. 101.

* * *

"But I tell you truly, there are some standing here who will not taste death before they see the kingdom of God" (Luke 9:27). See above, p. 68.

* * *

On the next day, when they had come down from the mountain, a great crowd met him. And behold, a man from the crowd cried, "Teacher, I beg you to look upon my son, for he is my only child; and behold, a spirit seizes him, and he suddenly cries out; it convulses him till he foams, and shatters him, and will hardly leave him. And I begged your disciples to cast it out, but they could not." Jesus answered, "O faithless and perverse generation, how long am I to be with you and bear with you? Bring your son here." While he was coming, the demon tore him and convulsed him. But Jesus rebuked the unclean spirit, and healed the boy, and gave him back to his father. And all were astonished at the majesty of God (Luke 9:37-43). See above, p. 70.

* * *

As they were going along the road, a man said to him, "I will follow you wherever you go." And Jesus said to him, "Foxes have holes, and birds of the air have nests: but the Son of man has nowhere to lay his head." To another he said, "Follow me." But he said, "Lord, let me first go and bury my father." But he said to him, "Leave the dead to bury their own dead; but as for you, go and proclaim the kingdom of God." Another said, "I will follow you, Lord; but let me first say farewell to those at my home." Jesus said to him, "No one who puts his hand to the plow and looks back is fit for the kingdom of God" (Luke 9:57-62). See above, p. 35.

* * *

NO parable strikes more sympathetic chords in people's hearts than that about the Good Samaritan. Like most parables, its message may be explained on a number of levels. A lawyer had asked Jesus what he must do to have eternal life and had received the answer to love God with all his heart and his neighbor as himself.

The passage reads:

> But he, desiring to justify himself, said to Jesus, "And who is my neighbor?" Jesus replied, "A man was going down from Jerusalem to Jericho, and he fell among robbers, who stripped him and beat him, and departed, leaving him half dead. Now by chance a priest was going down that road; and when he saw him he passed by on the other side. So likewise a Levite, when he came to the place and saw him, passed by on the other side. But a Samaritan, as he journeyed, came to where he was; and when he saw him, he had compassion, and went to him and bound up his wounds, pouring on oil and wine; then he set him on his own beast and brought him to an inn, and took care of him. And the next day he took out two denarii and gave them to the innkeeper, saying, 'Take care of him and whatever more you spend, I will repay you when I come back.' Which of these three, do you think, proved neighbor to the man who fell among the robbers?" He said, "The one who showed mercy on him." And Jesus said to him, "Go and do likewise" (Luke 10:29-37).

A Samaritan, a layman, not a minister, and furthermore, not even an orthodox Jew was the only passerby to show the wounded traveler compassion. Church fathers gave the parable both an allegorical and a practical application. In allegory, the traveler is Man, partly stripped and wounded by the Fall. Levitical sacrifices are unable to bring him aid, but our Lord, the Good Samaritan, rescues and restores him. (The English poet William Langland treats the parable in this manner in his *Vision of Piers Plowman*.) What tends to support this allegorical explanation is the fact that Christ never attacked priests and Levites, only scribes and Pharisees. Had he wished to hold up those men to scorn for their selfishness in failing to succor the wounded traveler, he would have made a scribe and a Pharisee the culprits.

That Christ did not have an ordinary, God-fearing Jew be the one who stops to assist the traveler but rather a Samaritan underscores his intention of having his audience accept the parable on its simplest level. He wished to teach love of neighbor as a responsibility or duty that overrides all other considerations. So the priest and Levite who might have avoided contact with the wounded traveler lest his body, if he were dead, or even his wounds, leave them ritually unclean—they passed him by on the other side of the road—are here subjected to Christ's criticism since love of neighbor should have taken precedence over any legal principle that might have been involved. The despised Samaritan, on the other hand, who was lowest of the low in the estimation of the Jews, instinctively knew what his duty was when he saw the fallen man, and he did it. Laws and conventions had not destroyed the natural sympathy that God had put into him. He did as Christ ordered: he loved his neighbor as he loved himself.

Oil and wine were believed to possess curative powers, oil for soothing pain or as an emollient, wine as a disinfectant.

* * *

HOUSEWIVES do not appreciate the story of Martha and Mary. The theologians of the Middle Ages who favored a symbolic interpretation of Scripture, offer them an explanation that they will find acceptable.

The passage reads:

> Now as they went on their way, he entered a village; and a woman named Martha received him into her house. And she had a sister called Mary, who sat at the Lord's feet and listened to his teaching. But Martha was distracted with much serving; and she went to him and said, "Lord, do you not care that my sister has left me to serve alone? Tell her then to help me." But the Lord answered her, "Martha, Martha, you are anxious and troubled about many things; one thing is needful. Mary has chosen the good portion, which shall not be taken away from her" (Luke 10:38-42).

This incident may have happened just as Luke describes it. One may hope that after Christ had said what he wished, or when Mary tired of listening, she would have gone inside and given Martha a hand. This story must have irked good housewives from the very beginnings of Christianity. Perhaps because of their urging, Martha came to be honored as the recognized sainted patroness of housewives and cooks as early as the fourth century.

It is not difficult to view Martha as the type of woman who always imagines there is much more to be done than is really necessary, and Mary, on the other hand, as one less inclined to see what is actually needed. Medieval writers honored both women, Martha as the symbol of the active spiritual life, Mary as representative of the contemplative.

Many commentators believe this Mary to be the Mary Magdalene spoken of by the evangelists in other connections, and both the women as sisters of the Lazarus whom Christ was later to raise from the dead.

*   *   *

"And I tell you, Ask, and it will be given you; seek, and you will find; knock, and it will be opened to you. For every one who asks receives, and he who seeks finds, and to him who knocks it will be opened. What father among you, if his son asks for a fish, will instead of a fish give him a serpent; or if he asks for an egg, will give him a scorpion? If you then, who are evil, know how to give good gifts to your children, how much more will the heavenly Father give the Holy Spirit to those who ask him!" (Luke 11:9-11). See above, p. 27.

See above, p. 27.

* * *

ONE would conclude that, on the basis of the gospels, Jesus took few occasions to make mention of his mother Mary. This one in Luke has invited varying interpretations.

The passage reads:

> As he said this, a woman in the crowd raised her voice and said to him, "Blessed is the womb that bore you, and the breasts that you sucked!" But he said, "Blessed rather are those who hear the word of God and keep it!" (Luke 11:27-28).

Some commentators detect an indirect slight to Mary in Christ's words, similar to that suggested in the reply he made when reminded that his mother and brothers were outside seeking him, namely, "Here are my mother and my brothers! For whoever does the will of my Father in heaven is my brother, and sister, and mother." (Matthew 12:49-50. See Luke 8:19-21, and above, p. 54.) Other commenators read into Christ's statement a double commendation for his mother, not only the fact that she was his mother but that she also heard his words and lived them. Both St. Augustine and St. Ambrose maintain that Mary was more blessed for believing the words of Christ than for actually being his mother. It has been suggested that Christ's response indicated he did not wish to accept any personal compliments for himself since the woman's praise was clearly meant for him.

* * *

"I tell you, my friends, do not fear those who kill the body, and after that have no more that they can do. But I will warn you whom to fear: fear him who, after he has killed, has power to cast into hell; yes, I tell you fear him! Are not five sparrows sold for two pennies? And not one of them is forgotten before God. Why, even the hairs of your head are all numbered. Fear not you are of more value than many sparrows" (Luke 12:4-7). See above, p. 45.

*   *   *

"And I tell you, everyone who acknowledges me before men, the Son of man also will acknowledge before the angels of God; but he who denies me before men will be denied before the angels of God. And every one who speaks a word against the Son of man will be forgiven; but he who blasphemes against the Holy Spirit will not be forgiven" (Luke 12:8-10). See above, p. 46.

*   *   *

"Do you think that I have come to give peace on earth? No, I tell you, but rather division; for henceforth in one house there will be five divided, three against two and two against three; they will be divided, father against son and son against father, mother against daughter and daughter against her mother, mother-in-law against her daughter-in-law and daughter-in-law against her mother-in-law" (Luke 12:51-53). See above, p. 46.

*   *   *

Now great multitudes accompanied him; and he turned and said to them, "If any one comes to me and does not hate his own father and mother and wife and children and brothers and sisters, yes, and even his own life, he cannot be my disciple. Whoever does not bear his own cross and come after me, cannot be my disciple" (Luke 14:25-27). See above, p. 46.

* * *

AMONG the more controversial parables is that which Christ told of the Prodigal Son. The fact that it lends itself to several applications or interpretations permits the individual to accept the one that appeals to him as the one Christ intended.

The passage reads:

And he said, "There was a man who had two sons; and the younger of them said to his father, 'Father, give me the share of property that falls to me.' And he divided his living between them. Not many days later, the younger son gathered all he had and took his journey into a far country, and there he squandered his property in loose living. And when he had spent everything, a great famine arose in that country, and he began to be in want. So he went and joined himself to one of the citizens of that country, who sent him into his fields to feed swine. And he would gladly have fed on the pods that the swine ate; and no one gave him anything. But when he came to himself he said, 'How many of my father's hired servants have bread enough and to spare, but I perish here with hunger! I will arise and go to my father, and I will say to him, "Father, I have sinned against heaven and before you; I am no longer worthy to be called your son; treat me as one of your hired servants." And he arose and came to his father. But while he was yet at a distance, his father saw him and had compassion, and ran and embraced him and kissed him. And the son said to him, 'Father, I have sinned against heaven and before you; I am no longer worthy to be called your son.' But the father said to his servants, 'Bring quickly the best robe, and put it on him; and put a ring on his hand, and shoes on his feet; and bring the fatted calf and kill it, and let us eat and make merry; for this my son was dead, and is alive again; he was lost, and is found.' And they began to make merry.

"Now his elder son was in the field; and as he came and drew near to the house, he heard music and dancing. And he called one of the servants and asked what this meant. And he said to him, 'Your brother has come, and your father has killed the fatted calf, because he has received him safe and sound.' But he was angry and refused to go in. His father came out and entreated him, but he answered his father, 'Lo, these many years I have served you, and I never disobeyed your command; yet you never gave me a kid, that I might make merry with my friends. But when this son of yours came, who has devoured your living with harlots, you killed for him the fatted calf!' And he said to him, 'Son, you are always with me, and all that is mine is yours. It was fitting to make merry and be glad, for this your brother was dead, and is alive; he was lost, and is found'" (Luke 15:11-32).

The parable of the Prodigal Son may be understood on three levels. The first, and probably the one Christ intended to be most evident, is that God is pleased with the repentance of a sinner. Just before telling of the prodigal son, Christ described how the woman with ten silver coins, losing one, searched unceasingly until she found the lost one, whereupon she called in her neighbors to celebrate with her. Then Christ went on to say, "Just so, I tell you, there is joy before the angels of God over one sinner who repents" (8-10). Next he spoke to the crowd of the prodigal son.

A second explanation on the human level affirms the

right of the father to welcome back a wayward son. The elder brother had actually lost nothing since the father assured him that all he possessed was his. If his steady work over the years had not brought him fattened calves and feasts, it had been no less appreciated.

A third explanation, this one on the allegorical level, presents the elder brother as representative of the Old Law, in a narrow sense the scribes and Pharisees, while the younger symbolized publicans and sinners, even Gentiles. The older brother, like the Pharisees, took much comfort in his self-righteousness, and even more perhaps in his ability to be able to condemn his less righteous brother.

Christ may also have nourished the hope that the Pharisees would interpret the parable as an invitation to them to come and claim their share of the Father's love and of the joys of heaven. Whatever the exact point(s) of the parable, Christ apparently left it to speak for itself. He offered no explanation, none, in any event, that the evangelist recorded.

*   *   *

NONE of Christ's parables has left more confusion in its wake than that of the Dishonest Servant or Unworthy Steward. Here is Luke's rendition of that difficult parable. The passage reads:

He also said to the disciples, "There was a rich man who had a steward, and charges were brought to him that this man was wasting his goods. And he called him and said to him, 'What is this that I hear about you? Turn in the account of your stewardship, for you can no longer be steward.' And the steward said to himself, 'What shall I do, since my master is taking the stewardship away from me? I am not strong enough to dig, and I am ashamed to beg. I have decided what to do, so that people may receive me into their houses when I am put out of the stewardship.' So, summoning his master's debtors, one by one, he said to the first, 'How much do you owe my master?' He said, 'A hundred measures of oil.' And he said to him, 'Take your bill, and sit down quickly and write fifty.' Then he said to another, 'And how much do you owe?' He said, 'A hundred measures of wheat.' He said to him, 'Take your bill and write eighty.' The master commended the dishonest steward for his shrewdness; for the sons of this world are more shrewd in dealing with their own generation than the sons of light. And I tell you, make friends for yourselves by means of unrighteous mammon, so that when it fails they may receive you into the eternal habitations" (Luke 16:1-10).

Perhaps no passage in all the gospels has occasioned more consternation among believers than this parable about the dishonest steward. Particularly disturbing have the faithful found Christ's admonition about using "unrighteous mammon" or the "mammon of iniquity" as the phrase appears in some older translations, to make friends who would, in return, provide them a welcome home in their eternal habitations.

Many commentators frankly confess their inability to explain away all the parable's problems even though the point of the story is quite clear. The steward, while dishonest, showed himself to be prudent while there was still time to be prudent. He made sure he had friends waiting to take care of him when he lost his job. Equally prudent should God-fearing people show themselves in preparing for their final home with God. The steward represented the children of this world who made provision for their later years. The people of God, the children of light, by contrast, are apt to neglect the preparation they should be making for their life after death. And the steward's master did not commend his servant for his dishonesty but for his prudence.

What complicates this essentially simple instruction is Christ's counsel to make use of "unrighteous mammon" (mammon of iniquity) in order to win friends who will provide a welcome in "the eternal habitations." What Christ is recommending is the use of material goods, money or property for example, which have no spiritual value in themselves but which man may use to advance a spiritual end: e.g., caring for the poor. The use of material goods must, however, be subordinated to a higher end since they are, in themselves, unrighteous mammon in comparison with true, eternal spiritual treasures. Christ bluntly affirmed this fact of spiritual life in the verses that followed: "No servant can serve two masters; for he will either hate the one and love the other, or he will be devoted to the one and despise the other. You cannot serve God and mammon" (16:13).

*   *   *

LUKE is the only evangelist who offers the parable about Dives and Lazarus, both wholly fictitious characters.

The passage reads:

"There was a rich man, who was clothed in purple and fine linen and who feasted sumptuously every day. And at his gate lay a poor man named Lazarus, full of sores, who desired to be fed with what fell from the rich man's table; moreover the dogs came and licked his sores. The poor man died and was carried by the angels to Abraham's bosom. The rich man also died and was buried; and in Hades, being in torment, he lifted up his eyes, and saw Abraham far off and Lazarus in his bosom. And he called out, 'Father Abraham, have mercy upon me, and send Lazarus to dip the end of his finger in water and cool my tongue; for I am in anguish in this flame.' But Abraham said, 'Son, remember that you in your lifetime received your good things, and Lazarus in like manner evil things; but now he is comforted here, and you are in anguish. And besides all this, between us and you a great chasm has been fixed, in order that those who would pass from here to you may not be able, and none may cross from there to us.' And he said, 'Then I beg you, father, to send him to my father's house, for I have five brothers, so that he may warn them, lest they also come into this place of torment.' But Abraham said, 'They have Moses and the prophets; let them hear them.' And he said, 'No, Father Abraham but if some one goes to them from the dead, they will repent.' He said to him, 'If they do not hear Moses and the prophets, neither will they be convinced if some one should rise from the dead' " (Luke 16:19-31).

As is the case with many of Christ's parables, this one possesses two levels of meaning, a human, direct, or literal application, and an allegorical interpretation. In its human application the story speaks for itself. The wealthy man while alive ignored any responsibility to the poor. In death he suffers punishment for his greed and negligence. His plea that Abraham send someone who had returned from the dead, like Lazarus, to warn his brothers to reform their way of living, is dismissed on the argument that they would ignore such a messenger just as they had refused to listen to Moses and the prophets.

This suggests the allegorical interpretation that is contained in the parable. Dives, as the rich man has been identified, along with his brothers, represent the Jews who had rejected Christ and the prophets who had foretold his coming.

* * *

The apostles said to the Lord, "Increase our faith!" And the Lord said, "If you had faith as a grain of mustard seed, you could say to this sycamore tree, 'Be rooted up, and be planted in the sea,' and it would obey you" (Luke 17:5-6). See above, p. 73.

* * *

A particularly well-known parable that only Luke records is the one about the Pharisee and the Publican.

The passage reads:

> He also told this parable to some who trusted in themselves that they were righteous and despised others: "Two men went up into the temple to pray, one a Pharisee and the other a tax collector. The Pharisee stood and prayed thus with himself, 'God, I thank thee that I am not like other men, extortioners, unjust, adulterers, or even like the tax collector. I fast twice a week, I give tithes of all that I get.' But the tax collector, standing far off, would not even lift up his eyes to heaven, but beat his breast, saying, 'God, be merciful to me a sinner!' I tell you, this man went down to his house justified rather than the other; for every one who exalts himself will be humbled, but he who humbles himself will be exalted" (Luke 18:9-14).

The sense of the parable is clear. While the tax collector was not as virtuous a man as the Pharisee, his attitude toward God was by far the more acceptable since no one, not even the virtuous person, may judge himself meritorious in the eyes of God. Some commentators propose an extension of the Pharisee to include the rich, proud Jews, the publican to represent the Gentiles.

* * *

And a ruler asked him, "Good Teacher, what shall I do to inherit eternal life?" And Jesus said to him, "Why do you call me good? No one is good but God alone" (Luke 18:18-19). See above, p. 107.

See above, p. 107.

* * *

Jesus looking at him said, "How hard it is for those who have riches to enter the kingdom of God! For it is easier for a camel to go through the eye of a needle than for a rich man to enter the kingdom of God." Those who heard it said, "Then who can be saved?" But he said, "What is impossible with men is possible with God" (Luke 18:24-27). See above, p. 78.

See above, p. 78.

* * *

"Then another came, saying, 'Lord, here is your pound, which I kept laid away in a napkin; for I was afraid of you, because you are a severe man; you take up what you did not lay down, and reap what you did not sow.' He said to him, 'I will condemn you out of your own mouth, you wicked servant! You knew that I was a severe man, taking up what I did not lay down and reaping what I did not sow. Why then did you not put my money into the bank, and at my coming I should have collected it with interest?' And he said to those who stood by, 'Take the pound from him, and give it to him who has the ten pounds.' (And they said to him, 'Lord, he has ten pounds!') 'I tell you, that to every one who has will more be given; but from him who has not, even what he has will be taken away'"(Luke 19:20-26). See above, p. 59.

See above, p. 59.

* * *

CHRIST often spoke to his disciples apart from the crowds, either to explain to them what he had preached to the public or to give them the kind of counsel that Luke records.

The passage reads:

"But before all this they will lay their hands on you and persecute you, delivering you up to the synagogues and prisons, and you will be brought before kings and governors for my name's sake. This will be a time for you to bear testimony. Settle it therefore in your minds, not to meditate beforehand how to answer; for I will give you a mouth and wisdom, which none of your adversaries will be able to withstand or contradict. You will be delivered up even by parents and brothers and kinsmen and friends, and some of you they will put to death; you will be hated by all for my name's sake. But not a hair of your head will perish. By your endurance you will gain your lives" (Luke 21:12-19). See above, p. 45.

The patent contradiction between "some of you they will put to death" and "not a hair of your head will perish" renders necessary a spiritual understanding of the latter assurance. In terms of spiritual values, Christ promised his disciples that even though they should suffer death, not a hair of their heads would suffer injury.

The most famous alleged historical instance of Christ's giving a persecuted person, through the instrumentality of the Holy Spirit, "a mouth and wisdom, which none of your adversaries will be able to withstand or contradict" is that of Joan of Arc before the episcopal tribunal which was trying her for heresy and witchcraft. Unfortunately, while Joan's judges were unable to "withstand or contradict" her eloquence, she died a martyr in the end, the same sort of death Christ is warning his followers they could expect. Joan remains France's most popular saint.

*   *   *

And he told them a parable: "Look at the fig tree, and all the trees; as soon as they come out in leaf, the summer is already near. So also, you see for yourselves and know that when you see these things taking place, you know that the kingdom of God is near. Truly, I say to you, this generation will not pass away till all has taken place. Heaven and earth will pass away, but my words will not pass away" (Luke 21:29-33). See above, p. 91.

*   *   *

ONE of the statements of Christ commonly overlooked in the reading of the Passion is his reference to two swords being sufficient. Luke gives the setting for Christ's puzzling remark.

The passage reads:

> And he said to them, "When I sent you out with no purse or bag or sandals, did you lack anything?" They said, "Nothing." He said to them, "But now, let him who has a purse take it, and likewise a bag. And let him who has no sword sell his mantle and buy one. For I tell you that this scripture must be fulfilled in me. 'And he was reckoned with transgressors'; for what is written about me has its fulfillment." And they said, "Look, Lord, here are two swords." And he said to them, "It is enough" (Luke 22:35-38).

Christ's direction to his disciples to take along their purses if they had one is out of character with the counsel he usually gave, e.g., "Take nothing for your journey, no staff, nor bag, nor bread, nor money" (Luke 9:3). Some commentators believe the imminence of his own suffering and death left Christ on the threshold of despair over the apparent failure of his mission. Perhaps half in seriousness, half in irony, he suggested to his disciples that, in view of the hostile world they would be encountering, a sword might be the best equipment to take with them, or possibly that two swords would be sufficient to cope with the danger immediately confronting them.

Commentators have had great difficulty with the reference to the sword and to Christ's cryptic statement, "It is enough." This last may have been a Hebrew formula amounting to our "Enough of this," in other words,

Christ's way of dismissing a subject which he found ridic-
ulous. He was no man of violence. Just a short time later,
in the garden of Gethsemane, he warned his disciples
against using force and he chided Peter for having cut off
the ear of the high priest's servant (see Luke 22:50-51, and
John 18:11). The phrase might also suggest that Christ,
again in control of himself after the impulsive (?) remark
about purchasing a sword, now felt his mission had been
accomplished, and the matter of the weapon should be dismissed.

While the entire episode about the sword(s) might have
held but passing interest for Christ and his disciples,
scholastics of the Middle Ages found great significance
therein. They agreed, in general, that the two swords
represented the two authorities in this life, the spiritual
(church) and the temporal (state). While most of them
were agreed that the spiritual authority was the higher
because of the simple fact that spiritual values stood above
material ones, they disagreed sharply over the question
whether the spiritual authority had the right to impose its
will in temporal (political) matters. They also disagreed as
to whether the church possessed both swords and simply
permitted the state to act as its representative with dele-
gated powers in temporal affairs. In a metaphysical sense,
the doctrine of the two swords lay at the root of the contest
between church and state in the Middle Ages.

THE GOSPEL ACCORDING TO JOHN

JOHN is the only evangelist who tells us about the wedding feast at Cana, the event that marked the beginning of Christ's ministry. Here is John's account of that incident. The passage reads:

On the third day there was a marriage at Cana in Galilee, and the mother of Jesus was there; Jesus also was invited to the marriage, with his disciples. When the wine gave out, the mother of Jesus said to him, "They have no wine." And Jesus said to her, "O woman, what have you to do with me? My hour has not yet come." His mother said to the servants, "Do whatever he tells you" (John 2:1-5).

Christ's answer to his mother, when she pointed out to him the lack of wine, is often judged harsh on two counts: first, the use of the word *woman*, and, second, the very abruptness of his answer: "O woman, what have you to do with me? My hour has not yet come."

That Jesus should call his mother *woman* and not mother suggests that he is now on his own and about to do the work of his father in heaven, therefore completely free of any maternal authority Mary might have wished to exercise. His statement that his time had not come implies that he was awaiting orders from the Father, as it were, and that until these had come he would do nothing. That Christ also used the term *woman* when addressing his mother on the cross (John 19:26) and again when speaking to Mary Magdalene after his resurrection (John 21:15), should rule out any suggestion of harshness or disrespect. (See also

Matthew 15:28, Luke 13:12, and John 4:21, for other instances of his use of the word *woman*.)

The statement, "What have you to do with me?" is the literal translation of a Semitic idiom and might better read, "What has this concern of yours to do with me?" It may also have the force of our "This is not our problem," or it may mean nothing more than a wish to be left in peace since his hour had not yet come. In any event, the effect of Christ's words, particularly since they were idiomatic, would have depended upon the tone with which they were spoken. Mary, at least, was not taken aback by them, but instructed the waiters, "Do whatever he tells you."

* * *

After this he went down to Capernaum, with his mother and his brothers and his disciples; and there they stayed for a few days (John 2:12). See above, p. 54.

* * *

DOES God punish men and women with physical sufferings who are guilty of sin? The Old Testament makes the connection between misfortune and sin patently clear: It is man's transgressions that bring God's anger and punishment upon him. John furnishes an episode that Christ might have employed to clarify that problem, but he did not.

The passage reads:

After this there was a feast of the Jews, and Jesus went up to Jerusalem. Now there is in Jerusalem by the Sheep Gate a pool, in Hebrew called Bethzatha, which has five porticoes. In these lay a multitude of invalids, blind, lame, paralyzed. One man was there, who had been ill for thirty-eight years. When Jesus saw him and knew that he had been lying there a long time, he said to him, "Do you want to be healed?" The sick man answered him, "Sir, I have no man to put me into the pool when the water is troubled, and while I am going another steps down before me." Jesus said to him, "Rise, take up your pallet, and walk." And at once the man was healed, and he took up his pallet and walked.

Now that day was the sabbath. So the Jews said to the man who was cured, "It is the sabbath, it is not lawful for you to carry your pallet." But he answered them, "The man who healed me said to me, 'Take up your pallet, and walk.'" They asked him, "Who is the man who said to you, 'Take up your pallet, and walk'?" Now the man who had been healed did not know who it was, for Jesus had withdrawn, as there was a crowd in the place. Afterward, Jesus found him in the temple, and said to him, "See, you are well! Sin no more, that nothing worse befall you." The man went away and told the Jews it was Jesus who had healed him (John 5:1-15).

The episode raises two issues of considerable importance: first, the implication that because of the man's sin, God had caused him to be paralyzed; second, that by curing the man on the Sabbath, Christ had violated the Mosaic law which prohibited work on that day.

As for the first issue, the major problem is the source of the man's paralysis. Some commentators conclude from Christ's warning to the man—worse might happen to him should he not stop sinning—that his paralysis had been a punishment for sin. This sin might have been some serious transgression committed thirty-eight years before, or his condition might simply be the consequence of a life of vice and dissipation. If the reasoning of those commentators who attribute the man's condition to some grave sin he had committed is correct, then Christ would have known that it was this sin that had led to the man's paralysis and have accordingly taken the occasion to warn him not to repeat what he had done.

Other commentators argue that Christ was using this occasion to impress upon the man the seriousness of sin without intending any suggestion that his former condition might have been the consequence of some moral transgression. A sympathetic critic might also reason, given the mysterious manner in which divine grace works, that God had used the man's paralysis, in itself only a physical evil, to bring about his conversion. Because of God's ability to bring good out of evil, the man's paralyzed condition had proved in the end to be the means of his spiritual regeneration. In support of the view that no sin had been involved in the man's paralysis, is Christ's answer to his disciples who had asked him whether the blindness of a certain man had been due to his sin or that of his parents. Christ assured them that sin had nothing to do with the blindness. (See John 9:3, and below, p. 152.)

The issue regarding Christ's attitude toward the Mosaic law that forbade work on the Sabbath must have been of special interest to the early Jewish Christians since the Jews generally observed that regulation. And if Christ in this instance did not flaunt his breaking of the law, they could discover several references in the writings of the evangelists when he had openly clashed with the Pharisees on this issue. He may in fact have deliberately violated the law in expectation of provoking an argument with them. Mark gives a description of one such instance.

> Again he entered the synagogue, and a man was there who had a withered hand. And they watched him, to see whether he would heal him on the sabbath, so that they might accuse him. And he said to the man who had the withered hand, "Come here." And he said to them, "Is it lawful on the sabbath to do good or to do harm, to save life or to kill?" But they were silent. And he looked around at them with anger, grieved at their hardness of heart, and said to the man, "Stretch out your hand." He stretched it out, and his hand was restored (3:1-5).

Christ's criticism of the position taken by the Pharisees about working on the Sabbath rose from several sources. He condemned them for their hypocrisy, for making such an ado about this regulation while at the same time demonstrating so little concern over moral values. During the course of one of his confrontations with them on this matter, he called them hypocrites. He had just cured a woman "who had had a spirit of infirmity for eighteen years; she was bent over and could not fully straighten herself." When the synagogue official, as spokesman for the Pharisees present, protested to Christ that he should do his healing on the six days of the week other than the Sabbath, he replied, "You hypocrites! Does not each of you on the sabbath untie his ox or his ass from the manger, and lead it away to water it?" (Luke 13:11, 14-15).

Christ would have insisted, had the argument proceeded any further, that what he did when he healed the crippled woman on the Sabbath was not working but a service, a benefit, an act of mercy. In this instance he accused them of inconsistency in that they would be willing to perform an act of mercy for a mere beast but not for a human being, a creature of God. "And ought not this woman, a daughter of Abraham whom Satan bound for eighteen years, be loosed from this bond on the sabbath?" (vs.16).

Though Christ was quite willing to respect the Mosaic law that prohibited work on the Sabbath, he did want that law to leave room for both works of mercy and of necessity. When the Pharisees voiced objection to the manner his disciples "plucked and ate some heads of grain, rubbing them in their hands," something they insisted violated the Sabbath, he not only justified their action on the basis of need, but announced quite frankly, "The Son of man is lord of the sabbath" (Luke 6:1,5). As the Son of man he not only had the right to declare what was lawful on the Sabbath and what was not, but also had the right to dispense with that obligation altogether had he chosen.

* * *

THE need to give Christ's words a figurative or symbolic interpretation or application is never greater than in this passage from John.

The passage reads:

"Your fathers ate the manna in the wilderness, and they died. This is the bread which comes down from heaven, that a man may eat of it and not die. I am the living bread which came down from heaven; if any one eats of this bread, he will live forever; and the bread which I shall give for the life of the world is my flesh" (John 6:49-51).

A literal understanding of the text would have Christ saying that the Hebrews who had eaten manna in the desert and had nevertheless died would not have died had they eaten the new bread from heaven. This bread would banish death. Christ could not have intended this statement to be taken literally since that interpretation would have placed all these people in hell.

The passage remains a difficult one. Perhaps John and the group of scholars with whom he was associated were willing to have Christ make this seemingly contradictory statement in order to enhance the unique preciousness of the "bread from heaven." The apparent contradiction would be lost upon most listeners, while the few who recognized it would have known what was meant. (See John 11:25-26, where Jesus assures Martha who is grieving over the death of her brother Lazarus: "I am the resurrection and the life; he who believes in me, though he die, yet shall he live, and whoever lives and believes in me shall never die.")

*   *   *

JOHN throws more light on the relationship between Christ and his "brothers." He also draws a clear distinction between Christ's "brothers" and his disciples.

The passage reads:

> After this Jesus went about in Galilee; he would not go about in Judea, because the Jews sought to kill him. Now the Jews' feast of Tabernacles was at hand. So his brothers said to him, "Leave here and go to Judea, that your disciples may see the works you are doing. For no man works in secret if he seeks to be known openly. If you do these things, show yourself to the world." For even his brothers did not believe in him (John 7:1-5).

For a consideration of the question whether Christ had brothers (and sisters), see above, p. 54. That his brothers (kinsmen) did not accept him, at least not prior to his resurrection, is suggested by Mark (3:21, 31-35). See also p. 46, for a reference to possible strife within Christ's own family circle over his preaching. The statement of the brothers, "If you do these things, show yourself to the world," may suggest that they did not believe he had worked any miracles.

* * *

JOHN offers another opportunity to biblical scholars to seek to analyze the problem raised above (p. 146) as to whether God punished sin here on earth.

The passage reads:

> As he passed by, he saw a man blind from his birth. And his disciples asked him, "Rabbi, who sinned, this man or his parents, that he was born blind?" Jesus answered, "It was not that this man sinned, or his parents, but that the works of God might be made manifest in him" (John 9:1-3).

The usual explanation given this passage is that the son was born blind through no fault either of his own or that of his parents. His blindness simply provided Christ the opportunity to work a miracle and thus prove his divinity and the infinite power of God. What about other persons born blind who were not miraculously cured? May one conclude that since Christ did not work a miracle in their case either they or their parents had sinned? Jesus does not bother to affirm or deny the assumption behind the question the disciples put to him, namely, whether it was the young man's fault or that of his parents. He limits his answer to this particular case.

The disciples with their questions were voicing a common belief, that is, that physical afflictions were the consequences of sin. See above, p. 146 and also Luke 13:1-5, where Christ warns his audience that unless they repented they would suffer the same fate as the eighteen on whom the tower at Siloam had fallen.

*   *   *

THE relationship between Father and Son was the most serious and persistent of several fundamental issues that confronted theologians during the early centuries of the church. Here is John's contribution to that problem, and a mighty important one it proved.

The passage reads:

> Philip said to him, "Lord, show us the Father, and we shall be satisfied." Jesus said to him, "Have I been with you so long, and yet you do not know me, Philip? He who has seen me has seen the Father; how can you say, 'Show us the Father?'" (John 14:8-9).

Philip's perplexity must have been shared by his fellow apostles and disciples. The nature of Christ and his relationship to the Father constituted the most divisive problem that faced the Christian church during the first five centuries of its existence. Even in this passage in which Christ insists that he and the Father were one, he assures his disciples that "I go to the Father" (vs. 12). According to the testimony of all four evangelists, Christ spoke repeatedly of the Father as apart and distinct from himself, the last time on the cross when he asked the Father why he had forsaken him. (See above, p. 94.)

Christ is telling Philip that whoever sees and believes him to be the son of God has already achieved his heavenly goal, which is to know and see God. He is also saying that he, the son, is himself as full a revelation of God as is available to man, that he is the image of God and that nothing more was necessary since he was the way and the truth and the life.

As far as Christ's mission on earth was concerned, he and the Father were indeed one. Christ's answer to Philip's question need not be interpreted as concealing any meta-physical implications regarding the precise relationship that existed between him and the Father.

*   *   *

PERHAPS the passage in John that biblical scholars have found most baffling is the manner he identifies the women at the foot of the cross.

The passage reads:

> But standing by the cross of Jesus were his mother, and his mother's sister, Mary the wife of Clopas, and Mary Magdalene. When Jesus saw his mother, and the disciple whom he loved standing near, he said to his mother, "Woman, behold, your son!" Then he said to the disciple, "Behold, your mother!" And from that hour the disciple took her to his own home (John 19:25-27).

If it were possible to identify precisely the women whom John places at the foot of the cross, it would help immensely in unraveling the question whether Christ actually had blood brothers or whether the brothers spoken of by the evangelists were simply kinsmen (cousins). (See above, p. 55.) If one accepts the view of Epiphanius and other church fathers that Joseph had children by an earlier wife who were then Christ's half-brothers and Mary's stepsons (see above, p. 56), it is easy to understand why Jesus, on the cross, might have preferred to give his mother into the care of his beloved disciple John. These "brothers" or "brethren" as they are referred to (see above, p. 54) had not accepted Christ's claims to be the Messiah and had engaged in bitter controversy with him. (See above, pp. 46, 64, 151.) John, the beloved disciple, might have been Christ's cousin if his mother Salome was Mary's sister.

Several commentators question the historicity of this passage since the three synoptic gospels, all of which preceded John's in time, say nothing about Mary's being present at the crucifixion. They simply speak of women, including Mary Magdalene and Mary, the mother of James the Younger and of Joses, and Salome, as viewing the crucifixion from a distance. (See Matthew 27:55-56; Mark 15:40; Luke 23:49, and above, p. 55.)

* * *

BIBLICAL scholars accept in stride the many duplications in the accounts the evangelists give about Christ and his ministry. When inconsistencies appear, as they do in their accounts of what happened after Christ's resurrection, that is another matter.

The passage in John reads:

> But Mary stood weeping outside the tomb, and as she wept she stooped to look into the tomb; and she saw two angels in white, sitting where the body of Jesus had lain, one at the head and one at the feet. They said to her, "Woman, why are you weeping?" She said to them, "Because they have taken away my Lord, and I do not know where they have laid him." Saying this, she turned round and saw Jesus standing, but she did not know that it was Jesus. Jesus said to her, "Woman, why are you weeping? Whom do you seek?" Supposing him to be the gardener, she said to him, "Sir, if you have carried him away, tell me where you have laid him, and I will take him away." Jesus said to her, "Mary." She turned and said to him in Hebrew, "Rabboni!" (which means Teacher). Jesus said to her, "Do not hold me, for I have not yet ascended to the Father; but go to my brethren and say to them, I am ascending to my Father and your Father, to my God and your God." Mary Magdalene went and said to the disciples, "I have seen the Lord"; and she told them that he had said these things to her (John 20:11-18).

There exists a measure of inconsistency among the accounts as given by the four evangelists concerning the circumstances following upon Christ's resurrection. Matthew writes that Mary Magdalene and the other Mary (Salome) came to examine the tomb on the Sunday morning following the crucifixion, only to be told by the angel that Christ had already risen and that they should go and so inform his disciples. Then as they were on their way Christ met them and made himself known to them, whereupon "they came up and took hold of his feet and worshipped him" (Matthew 28:9). This account does not accord with John's version which has Christ meeting only Mary Magdalene whom he cautioned, "Do not hold me."

Several explanations or solutions to the problem have been offered. A slight alteration of the text in John would have this read, "Do not be afraid," instead of "Do not hold me." If one stays with "Do not hold me," a suggested explanation is that Mary Magdalene was clinging to Jesus for fear of losing him again, and that he had reassured her that she had no reason to fear that as yet. To translate the Greek into "Do not touch me" as the words appear in a number of English versions would make it difficult to explain the above passage in Matthew where the women clasp Jesus' feet without his remonstrating, or with Christ's order to Thomas a week later that he put his hands to the marks in his hands and into his side (John 20:27). The passage retains its problems.

BIBLIOGRAPHY

Achtemeier, Paul J., *Invitation to Mark*. Doubleday &
Company, Inc. Garden City, N.Y., 1978.

Alford, Henry, *The New Testament for English Readers*.
Moody Press. Chicago, 1955.

Allen, W. C., *A Critical and Exegetical Commentary on
the Gospel according to S. Matthew*. T. & T. Clark.
Edinburgh, 1957.

Anchor Bible, The. The Gospel According to John. Translation and Notes by Raymond E. Brown. 2 vols.
Doubleday & Company, Inc. Garden City, N.Y.,
1970. *The Gospel According to Matthew*. Translation
and Notes by W. F. Albright & C. S. Mann. Doubleday & Company, Inc. Garden City, N.Y., 1971.

Argyle, A. W., *The Gospel According to Matthew*. University Press. Cambridge, 1963.

Barnes, Albert, *Barnes' Notes on the New Testament*.
Kregel Publications. Grand Rapids, Mich., 1966.

Beare, Francis Wright, *The Earliest Records of Jesus*.
Abingdon Press. New York, 1962.

Bernard, J. H., *A Critical and Exegetical Commentary on
the Gospel According to St. John*. 2 vols. T. & T.
Clark. Edinburgh, 1962-3.

Best, Ernest, "Mark iii, 21, 21, 31-35," *New Testament
Studies,* XXII (1976), pp. 309-319.

Bowman, John, *The Gospel of Mark*. E. J. Brill. Leiden,
1965.

Brown, Raymond E., *Jesus: God and Man*. Bruce Publishing Co. Milwaukee, 1967. *New Testament Essays*.
Doubleday & Company, Inc. Garden City, N.Y.,
1968. *The Birth of the Messiah*. Doubleday & Company, Inc. Garden City, N.Y., 1977.

Bultmann, Rudolf, *The Gospel of John.* A Commentary. Westminster Press. Philadelphia, 1971.

Burkill, T. A., *New Light on the Earliest Gospel.* Cornell University Press. Ithaca, N.Y., 1972.

Campbell, W. K. Lowther, *Concise Bible Commentary.* Macmillan Co. New York, 1953.

Davies, W. D., *Invitation to the New Testament.* Doubleday & Company, Inc. Garden City, N.Y., 1966.

Drury, John, *The Gospel of Luke.* Macmillan Co. New York, 1973

Easton, Burton Scott, *The Gospel According to St. Luke.* Charles Scribner's Sons. New York, 1926.

Filson, Floyd, *A Commentary on the Gospel According to St. Matthew.* Harper & Row. New York, 1960.

Gould, Ezra, *A Critical and Exegetical Commentary on the Gospel According to St. Mark.* T. & T. Clark. Edinburgh, 1961.

Harrington, Wilfrid J., *Explaining the Gospels.* Paulist Press. New York, 1963. *Key to the Bible: Record of Revelation: The Old Testament: The New Testament.* 3 vols. Doubleday & Company, Inc. Garden City, N.Y., 1976.

Hoskyns, Edwyn, *The Fourth Gospel.* Faber & Faber. London, 1956.

Interpreter's Bible. 12 vols. Abingdon Press. New York, 1951-7.

Jerome Biblical Commentary, The, Eds. Raymond E. Brown, Joseph A. Fitzmyer, Roland E. Murphy. Prentice-Hall, Inc. Englewood Cliffs, N.J., 1968.

Johnson, Sherman, *A Commentary on the Gospel According to St. Mark.* Harper & Row. New York, 1960.

Jones, G. V., *The Art and Truth of the Parables.* S.P.C.K. London, 1964.

Karris, Robert J., *Invitation to Luke*. Doubleday & Company, Inc. Garden City, N.Y., 1977

Knox, Ronald, *A Commentary on the Gospels*. Sheed and Ward. New York, 1954.

Ladd, George Eldon, *A Theology of the New Testament*. Eerdmans. Grand Rapids, Mich., 1974.

Lambrecht, J., "The Relatives of Jesus in Mark," *Novum Testamentum,* XVI (1974), pp. 241–58.

Leaney, A. R. C., *A Commentary on the Gospel According to St. Luke*. Harper & Row. New York, 1958.

Lightfoot, J. B., *Saint Paul's Epistle To the Galatians*. Macmillan. London, 1921.

Lightfoot, R. H., *St. John's Gospel*. A Commentary. Ed. C. F. Evans. Oxford University Press. London, 1960.

Macrae, George W., *Invitation to John*. Doubleday & Company, Inc. Garden City, N.Y., 1978.

Marsh, John, *The Gospel of St. John*. Penguin Books. Baltimore, 1968.

Marxsen, W., *Introduction to the New Testament*. Tr. G. Buswell. Fortress Press. Philadelphia, 1968.

Mary in the New Testament, Eds. Raymond E. Brown et al. Paulist Press. New York, 1978.

McHugh, J., *The Mother of Jesus in the New Testament*. Doubleday & Company, Inc. Garden City, N.Y., 1975.

McKenzie, John L., *The Power and the Wisdom*. Bruce Publishing Co. Milwaukee, 1965.

McNeille, A. H., *An Introduction to the Study of the New Testament*. Clarendon Press. Oxford, 1953.

Montefiore, C. J. G., *The Synoptic Gospels*. 2 vols. KTAV Pub. House, Inc. New York, 1968

Moule, C. F. D., *The Birth of the New Testament*. Harper & Row. New York, 1962.

Neill, Stephen, *The Interpretation of the New Testament.* Oxford University Press. London, 1964.

New Bible Commentary (Revised). Ed. D. Guthrie & J. A. Motyer, Eerdmans. Grand Rapids, Mich., 1970.

New Catholic Commentary on Holy Scripture, The (Revised). Thomas Nelson, Inc. Publishers. Nashville and New York, 1975.

New Catholic Encyclopedia. 16 vols. McGraw-Hill. New York, 1967–74.

New Oxford Annotated Bible with the Apocrypha, The (Revised). Ed. Herbert G. May and Bruce M. Metzger. Oxford Unversity Press. New York, 1973.

Nineham, D. E., *The Gospel of St. Mark.* Westminster Press. Philadelphia, 1977.

Plummer, Alfred, *A Critical and Exegetical Commentary on the Gospel According to S. Luke.* T. & T. Clark, Edinburgh, 1960.

Rahner, Karl, *Mary Mother of the Lord.* Herder and Herder. New York, 1963.

Richardson, A., *The Gospel According to Saint John.* SCM. London, 1959.

Rigaux, Beda, *The Testimony of St. Matthew.* Tr. Paul Joseph Oligny. Franciscan Herald Press. Chicago, 1968.

———, *The Testimony of St. Mark.* Tr. Malachy Carroll. Franciscan Herald Press. Chicago, 1966.

Sanders, Joseph N., *A Commentary on the Gospel Accord- to St. John.* Harper & Row. New York, 1968.

Schnackenburg, Rudolf, *The Gospel According to St. John.* Tr. Kevin Smyth. Herder and Herder. New York, 1968.

Streeter, Burnett Hillman, *The Four Gospels.* Macmillan Co. New York, 1925.

Taylor, Vincent, *The Names of Jesus*. St. Martin's Press. New York, 1959.

——, *The Gospel According to St. Mark*. St. Martin's Press. New York, 1972.

Thompson, G. H. P., *The Gospel According to Luke*. Clarendon Press. Oxford, 1972.

Tinsley, E. J., *The Gospel According to Luke*. University Press. Cambridge, 1974.

Vawter, Bruce, *The Four Gospels: An Introduction*. Doubleday & Company, Inc. Garden City, N.Y., 1967.

INDEX OF GOSPEL PASSAGES

INDEX OF PUZZLING PASSAGES